WRITING BETTER LYRICS

WRITING
BETTER
LYRICS

PAT PATTISON

WRITER'S DIGEST BOOKS
CINCINNATI, OHIO

ABOUT THE AUTHOR

Pat Pattison is a professor of music and songwriting at the Berklee College of Music in Boston. He developed the curriculum for Berklee's songwriting major—the first of its kind anywhere—and frequently conducts songwriting workshops around the United States. He is the author of *Managing Lyric Structure* and *Rhyming Techniques and Strategies,* and was a regular contributor to *Home and Studio Recording Magazine.* He lives in North Hampton, New Hampshire.

Writing Better Lyrics. Copyright © 1995 by Pat Pattison. Printed and bound in the United States of America. All rights reserved. No part of this book may be reproduced in any form or by any electronic or mechanical means including information storage and retrieval systems without permission in writing from the publisher, except by a reviewer, who may quote brief passages in a review. Published by Writer's Digest Books, an imprint of F&W Publications, Inc., 1507 Dana Avenue, Cincinnati, Ohio 45207. (800) 289-0963. First edition.

This hardcover edition of *Writing Better Lyrics* features a "self-jacket" that eliminates the need for a separate dust jacket. It provides sturdy protection for your book while it saves paper, trees and energy.

Other fine Writer's Digest Books are available from your local bookstore or direct from the publisher.

00 99 98 97 96   6 5 4 3 2

Library of Congress Cataloging-in-Publication Data

Pattison, Pat
    Writing better lyrics / by Pat Pattison.—1st ed.
      p.   cm.
    Includes index.
    ISBN 0-89879-682-2
    1. Lyric writing (Popular music). I. Title.
MT67.P383   1995
782.42164'0268—dc20   95-20964
                                                  CIP

Edited by Julie Wesling Whaley
Designed by Brian Roeth

The permissions on page vi-vii constitute an extension of this copyright page.

Thanks

To my students, especially those who have allowed me to include their work in this book. Facing their creativity, questions and desire always challenges me and requires me to look further to make sure I get it right.

To my fellow faculty at Berklee College of Music for trying out these ideas and making them work; for their support, suggestions and insights.

To the writers and publishers who allowed me to include such excellent material, especially Beth Nielsen Chapman and Janis Ian for their interest and encouragement.

To Mike Reid for his enthusiasm, and for diving into Object Writing with such passion.

To Gillian, Melissa, Kami, Rob, Lynn, Dave, Lee, and a host of other Berklee transplants to Nashville, New York and Los Angeles for proving that this stuff works.

To my son Jason.

I especially want to thank Susan Benjamin for her encouragement, for editing the original articles, and for her comments, focus and inspiration; in short, for making this book possible.

ACKNOWLEDGMENTS

SOME PEOPLE'S LIVES by Janis Ian and Kye Fleming. © Copyright 1986 Irving Music Inc. and Eaglewood Music (BMI) and MCA Music Publishing, A Division of MCA Inc. and Taosongs. All Rights Administered by Almo-Irving Music Inc. (BMI) on Behalf of Eaglewood Music for the World. All Rights Reserved. International © Secured. Used by permission.

BETWEEN FATHERS AND SONS by John Jarvis and Gary Nicholson. © Copyright 1986 Tree Publishing Co., Inc. and Cross Keys Publishing Co., Inc. All rights administered by Sony Music Publishing, 8 Music Square West, Nashville TN 37203. All Rights Reserved. Used by permission.

TOP OF THE ROLLER COASTER Words and Music by David Wilcox. © Copyright 1991 Irving Music Inc. and Ocean Bonfire Music (BMI). All Rights Administered by Irving Music, Inc. (BMI). All Rights Reserved. International Copyright Secured. Used by permission.

CHILD AGAIN by Beth Nielsen Chapman. © Copyright 1987, 1990 BMG Songs Inc. (ASCAP). All Rights Reserved. Used by permission.

THE GREAT PRETENDER by Buck Ram. © Copyright 1955 by Panther Music Corp. Copyright Renewed.

SLOW HEALING HEART by Jim Rushing. © Copyright 1984 Maypop Music (a division of Wildcountry, Inc.) (BMI). All Rights Reserved. Used by permission.

STILL CRAZY AFTER ALL THESE YEARS by Paul Simon. © Copyright 1974. Used by permission of the Publisher.

TRAIN IN THE DISTANCE by Paul Simon. © Copyright 1981. Used by permission of the Publisher.

THE FIRE INSIDE by Bob Seger. © Copyright 1988, 1991. Gear Publishing Co. All Rights Reserved. Used by Permission.

YEARS by Beth Neilsen Chapman. © Copyright 1987. Warner-Tamerlane Publishing Corp. All Rights Reserved. Used by Permission.

GIVE ME WINGS Words and Music by Don Schlitz and Rhonda Fleming © Copyright 1986 by MCA Music Publishing, A Division of MCA Inc., Don Schlitz Music, Irving Music and Eaglewood Music, 1755 Broadway, New York, NY 10019

EYE OF THE HURRICANE Words and Music by David Wilcox. © Copyright 1989 by Irving Music Inc. and Midnight Ocean Bonfire Music (BMI). All Rights Administered by Irving Music, Inc. (BMI). All Rights Reserved, International © Secured. Used by permission.

THE END OF THE INNOCENCE by Don Henley, Bruce Hornsby. © Copy-

TABLE OF CONTENTS

INTRODUCTION

Much of the material in this book originally appeared as articles in *Recording Magazine* under the title *Better Lyrics Through Science*. I am grateful to the editors for giving me a forum to try my ideas out. Some of the material has also appeared in the LASS *Musepaper* and in *The Performing Songwriter* magazine.

The book divides, generally, into two topics: generating lyric ideas, and organizing them effectively. Chapters one through three cover brainstorming techniques for generating ideas. The rest of the book shows you what to do with them: developing verses and managing repetition, handling point of view, and organizing ideas into effective form. The final chapter is an overview linking all the techniques together into one process.

Take your time as you read through the book. Do the exercises wherever they occur. When I repeat a lyric in its entirety, though I may have changed only portions of it to illustrate a point, read it through carefully. Involve yourself in the world of the lyric each time to see how changes resonate through its entirety.

It's like being a high jumper on a track team. You already have the natural ability to jump pretty high, so you *could* content yourself with the same height you've always jumped. But if you had a desire to get better, to perfect yourself—to get the most you possibly can out of your talents, how would you go about it? The best way is piece by piece. Slow.

Your coach takes you into the film room to look at films of some of the best jumpers ever. You watch them in real time and can't believe what you're seeing. How can anyone do that? Your first impulse is to walk out, contenting yourself with what now seem like measly little jumps; better yet, go lie on the beach and do nothing. Ugh!

Then the coach slows the film down: "Watch the approach. How many steps? Where is the acceleration, the turn, the takeoff? Look at the leading arm, the trailing leg."

As you watch, you realize that, step by step, you understand what's going on. You could do most of that stuff if you worked at it. With some focused practice, you could at least jump higher than you do. Maybe not a world record, but better than third in the next regional meet would be a good start.

Slow the process down, look at it frame by frame, and learn all the moves. Figure out which muscles are involved, then try each one. Some of your muscles may already be equal to the task, but others will need development. Work on the various machines in the exercise room. Isolate the muscles that need work and develop them—for strength, for flexibility. Each one must be ready for its job in the dance over the bar.

Then practice each of the moves, separately. Measure your steps as you approach the bar. How far back do you start to get to the perfect takeoff point? Do it over and over until your muscles learn it and you can do it automatically. Head for the swimming pool to practice the turn, the lift, the arch and the kick. Over and over, slowly, in water that holds you up and lets your muscles memorize their moves.

Finally, put all the moves together. First in the swimming pool where you can keep the process slow, allowing your muscles to link the moves together and get the feeling into your muscle memory, then at last, out in the summer air.

Real time is a breeze after you've slowed the process down. You'll recognize each part as it goes by. And when things aren't quite right, you'll know what to work on because you understand the process move by move.

Take your time. You'll only get better.

Chapter One

Object Writing
The Art of the Diver

The native dives deep into the waters of his bay, holding his breath to reach the soft pink and blue glow below. Sleek through the water, churning up no cloud to disturb the bottom, he stretches and he opens the shell. Rising to the surface he holds it aloft and shimmering in the sun: mother of all pearls, breathing light.

Like his pearl, your best writing lies somewhere deep within. It glows in fresh, interesting colors no one ever imagined in exactly that way before. Your most important job as a writer is to master the art of diving to those deep places, for there and only there you will find your own unique writing voice.

Remember this fundamental fact: You are absolutely unique. There never was, is not now, nor ever can be anyone exactly like you. The proof lies in the vaults of your senses, where you have been storing your sense memories all your life. They have come cascading in through your senses, randomly and mostly unnoticed, sinking to the bottom. Learn to dive for them. When you recover one, when you rise with it to the surface and hold it aloft, you will not only surprise your onlookers, you will surprise yourself.

Much of lyric writing is technical: the stronger your skills are, the better you can express your creative ideas. You must spend time on the technical areas of lyric writing like rhyme, rhythm, contrast, balance and repetition. Here I want to focus on the most important part of all creative writing, and therefore surely of lyric writing, the art of deep diving: finding your own unique voice and vision.

OBJECT WRITING

The best diving technique I know is Object Writing. It's direct and simple. You arbitrarily pick an object—a *real* object—and focus your senses on it. Treat the object as a diving board to launch you inward to the vaults of your senses.

Although you understand your five senses, you could probably stand a few exercises to sharpen them, especially the four you don't normally use when you write. If I asked you to describe the room you're in, your answer would be primarily, if not completely, visual. Try spending a little time alone with each sense. What's there? How does the kitchen table smell? How would the rug feel if you rubbed your bare back on it? How big does the room sound? (If it were twice as big? Half as big?) How would the table taste if you licked it? No, it's not silly. Remember this, it is important: The more senses you incorporate into your writing, the better it breathes and dances.

You have two additional senses that may need a little explanation.

1. Organic sense is your awareness of inner bodily functions, for example, heartbeat, pulse, muscle tension, stomach aches, cramps, breathing. Athletes are most keenly focused on this sense, but you use it constantly, especially in responsive situations. I've been sitting here writing too long. I need a back rub.
2. Kinesthetic sense is, roughly, your sense of relation to the world around you. When you get seasick or drunk, the world around you blurs—like blurred vision. When the train you're on is standing still and the one next to it moves, your kinesthetic sense goes crazy. Children spin, roll down hills, or ride on tilt-a-whirls to stimulate this sense. Dancers and divers develop it most fully—they look onto a stage or down to the water and see spatial possibilities for their bodies. It makes me dizzy just thinking about it.

EXERCISE

Pick an object at random and write about it. Dive into your sense memories and associations surrounding the object. Anything goes, as long as it is sense-bound. Write freely. No rhythm, no rhyme. No need for complete sentences. Use all seven senses: sight, hearing, smell, taste, touch, organic and kinesthetic. Like this:

Back Porch

I must have been four. Memories from that time are a rare species— lobbing in like huge bumblebees on transparent wings, buzzing old Remington shavers torn free from those thick and brittle wires tangled in webs under our porch where I loved to crawl and hide; black snaking wires disappearing up through floors and humming into wall and socket. I still hear them.

I hid under the back porch, smell of damp summer earth cool under my hands, ducking, scrunching my shoulders tight to avoid the rusty nails waiting patiently above for my back or skull to forget them. The tingling along my back and neck kept reminding me, don't stand up.

Under the back porch, a place tinged with danger and smelling of earth, the air tastes faintly of mold and hollyhocks twining around the trellises that I see only the bottoms of, speckled gold by the shafts of sun slipping through high elm branches in the backyard, weaving shadows like Grandma's lace dresser doilies. When I squint, I can blur the sunlight into a bridge of green-gold. Crouching there fetal and content, I could feel Mom above me, could hear her high heels tap-tapping.

No one else has ever associated exactly those experiences with "back porch," yet anyone can understand them, relate to them. Because they are drawn from senses, they will stimulate your senses. You will draw from your own sense reservoir, making my experiences yours. They take on a new look traveling from me into you. They get filtered through your senses and memories. They add to your uniqueness.

Look at the sense information in *Back Porch*:

Sight: huge bumblebees on transparent wings; thick and brittle wires tangled in webs; black snaking wires disappearing up through floors; rusty nails; hollyhocks twining around the trellises I see only the bottoms of; speckled gold by shafts of sun; high elm branches in the backyard; weaving shadows like Grandma's lace dresser doilies; When I squint, I can blur the sunlight into a bridge of green-gold

Hearing: buzzing old Remington shavers; humming into wall and socket. I still hear them; could hear her high heels tap-tapping

Smell: smell of damp summer earth smelling of earth

Taste: the air tastes faintly of mold and hollyhocks

Touch: thick and brittle wires; damp summer earth cool under my hands; tingling along my back and neck

Organic: crawl; crouching; ducking, scrunching shoulders tight; stand up quick; tingling along my back and neck; When I squint; crouching there fetal and content

Kinesthetic: lobbing in; tingling along my back and neck kept reminding me; avoid rusty nails waiting patiently above for my back or skull to forget them; don't stand up; I could feel Mom above me

TEN AND ONLY TEN MINUTES—A.M.

Object Writing works best when you do it for ten minutes, first thing in the morning. Yes, I know—I'm brain-dead then too. But you can always find ten minutes just by getting up a tad earlier, and the effort will pay huge dividends.

Two beings inhabit your body: you, who stumbles groggily to the coffeepot to start another day, and the writer in you, who could remain blissfully asleep and unaware for days, months, even years as you go on about your business. If your writer is anything like mine, "lazy," even "slug" is too kind. Always wake up your writer early, so you can spend the day together. It's amazing the fun the two of you can have watching the world go by. Your writer will be active beside you, sniffing and tasting, snooping for metaphors. It's like writing all day without moving your fingers.

If, instead, you waited until evening to wake your writer up, you'd float through the day alone, missing the wonderful worlds your writer sees. Old lazybones, meanwhile, would get up late and retire early.

Guarantee yourself ten minutes and *only* ten minutes. Set a timer, and stop the second it goes off. You're much more likely to sit down to a clearly limited commitment. But be sure you always stop at the buzzer. If you get on a roll some morning and let yourself write for thirty minutes, guess what you'll say the next morning:

1. "Ugh, I don't have the energy to do it this morning (remembering how much energy you spent yesterday), and besides,

2. I've already written my ten minutes for the next two days. I'll start again Thursday."

That's how most people stop morning writing altogether. Any good coach will tell you that more is gained practicing a short time each day than doing it all at once. Living with it day by day keeps writing on your mind and in your muscles.

Soon something like this will happen: at minute six you'll really get on a roll, diving, plunging, heading directly for the soft pink and blue glow below when, *beep!* the timer goes off. Just stop. Wherever you are. Stop. *Writus interruptus.* All day your frustrated writer will grumble "Boy, what I might have said if you hadn't stopped me." Guaranteed, when you sit down the next morning, you will dive deeper faster. The bottom in three minutes flat. Next time, one minute. Finally, instantly. That is your goal: immediate access—speed and depth. So much information and experience tumbles by every minute of your life, the faster you can explore each bit, the faster you can sample the next. But, of course, speed doesn't count without depth. The ten minute absolute limit is the key to building both. And it guarantees a manageable task.

Object writing prepares you for whatever other writing you do. It is not a substitute.

GROUP WRITING

Object Writing is great for a group. It's fascinating to hear other writers dive and roll off the same object. Get some people together, set a timer, then point to someone: "Pick an object." "Popsicle." Boom, you're all off. When time is up, each person reads. In larger groups (five to ten), shorten the time to five minutes so that, during readings, no one gets impatient. Do two or three at a sitting. Each one will be better because you feed off each other—each of you has something unique to offer. In a good group, the level of writing gets very high (or deep) very quickly. With smaller groups, write eight to ten minutes each time (never longer). Remember though, pick *real* objects. Butter. Canary. The smell of split pea soup. Hanging ivy. Hot coffee.

Here is an example of group Object Writing, done by Berklee College of Music students. Before you read it, stop. Set a timer for ten minutes and write on *holding my breath*. The only rule is to stay bound to your senses. Then read on.

Holding My Breath

High above me, right underneath the red and green canvas of the big top stands a little teeny man on a platform the size of a postage stamp. The ringmaster's voice booms and the crowd snaps to attention. He talks about the little man way up high among the spider web ropes. The crowd "oohs" and "aahs" like a locomotive gathering steam. My chest tightens as the ringmaster points to a big tub of water underneath the little man's platform. An iceball of fear forms in my stomach as I realize that the big bad ringmaster in his demon black cape is making the little man jump from oh-so-high-up-there into not enough water to fill my Snoopy wading pool.

I start to tremble and my chest hurts. I shut my eyes tight wanting to scream to my father, "Stop the bad man! Stop the bad man!" I feel the crowd stop breathing around me, like the earth stopping its rotation.

I hear a tremendous splash and the iceball inside me bursts into millions of shards and my breath explodes out like a horse snorting.
—Gene Hafner

The water's clarity startles me. How deep is it really—looks like just a few feet. I see a small stone glittering an orange-gold as the ripples move slightly. The water is warm—I decide to dive in just for fun to reach the stone. My body feels warm, covered, hugged by the water—deeper and deeper I go—eyes open, stinging—just a little farther ahead the stone urges me deeper than I thought—maybe ten feet maybe more—my ears hurt from the pressure. I reach the bottom—see the stone, grab its roundness and push off toward the sunlight overhead. I notice now I'm holding my breath and the pain I feel is causing some panic. Thoughts begin to flash like headlights on the highway. I see myself in my apartment practicing voice—holding my breath—straining to hold the notes—chest up, lungs expanded— My push was not strong enough to break the glassy surface still high above. Imprisoned in light, I see above and beneath so clearly. All is gone, I can't hold the note any longer—I gasp for breath—water rushes in fills the empty caverns of my lungs. The precious stone falls from my grip—rolls featherlight—lands on the bottom.—Robin Richardson

Without the effort of my skin I hope to be more alive, less in the way of things; more to the marrow; less a jumbled matrix of silver bones and angled protuberances—I too have been holding my breath wrong all my life—my chest contracts; ribs puncture sack cloth and I am an instrument of habits no longer useful but oh so heavy, like granite, my neck burrows down into the steaming cavern of misuse and ignored valuables. The ringing click of tubes and pipes and hollow bells could suffocate me.

I have been a willful storm, an isolated princess, crystal lattice and non-frame easily punctured—today I have lost my shape—like the green seaweed, the bubbles attached. The mangy surfaces of weeds. There are only sharp colors around me—I have flopped into this position late, maybe, but one card is a slick expression of possibilities if only I believe it right now.—Laura Siersema

The balloon stretched tighter, the rubber skin taut almost to breaking. Tying it, I let it away; a playful, yellow sphere that bounced off holding my breath, my gift. Minutes earlier it had given me its gift of helium, a passing rush, elated high. The helium didn't last long. It was gone as soon as it was mine. My gift will last longer; days, maybe a week. Which gift was better, I wondered as I watched the balloon run with a gust of wind. Both and neither I suppose.—Gerry Diamond

Try two-way Object Writing with someone whose writing you really like. You can do it over the phone. Call and say: "Got ten minutes? Good. You wanna pick, or should I? Bacon fat? OK, go!" Hang up, then call back in ten minutes and read to each other. Do you have a three-way hookup? Even better. (By the way, this is a great way to find co-writers without actually committing yourselves to a song. You can get to know each other slowly. If it doesn't click, you've still exercised your divers.)

EXERCISE

Here's another batch from a group of Nashville songwriters, some with publishing deals. Set your timer. Ready? *Polyester.* Go.

Polyester

Thick and fibery you can see the patterns of rows on houndstooth or big flowers—it is porous and yet when I wore that nasty jumpsuit

my mother made me, I felt as if I couldn't breathe; sweat that had no place to go, sitting stagnant on my skin, imprisoned by polyester. Who is Polly? Who is Ester? Were they the two old women who invented this poor excuse for a garment? I sit on my grandmother's lap, gazing at the sheen on her plump legs wrapped in hosiery—feeling the uneasiness of my polyester against hers, and though I love her, it is gross. My head rests on her collar which is doused with Chantilly and a slight hint of hair spray. I stare at her jaw as it moves gabbing up and down, her voice loud and resonant with my ear to her chest—it is nice to have her here but she hugs so tight—too tight—and she says "Oh Dahhlin" and "bless yoah heart" . . . But she would wear those dresses, I wore the jumpsuits, we all were prisoners to that fabulous fabric of the seventies.—April McLean

Lillie Dorholt had orange hair and orange lips and an orange voice and a big box of clothes for me. Pity clothes. You poor girl, look at you, you look like a welfare boy clothes. How's the divorce treatin' ya clothes. My mom's best coffee friend since before I was born, visiting us at the new house, bringing me a box of 14 karat, 100 proof, brand-stretching new 'yester from a children's sample sale. Purple was the theme. Purple stretch pants with the white vertical patterns all the way down to the gently flaring ankles. Purple itchy shirts, short sleeved with extra itchy turtlenecks in case you're hot and cold at the same time. The purple clothes that filled the box became the purple snapshots of me at the state fair, blonde hair volcano-ing at the top of head, fists around the steering wheel of a boat, an orange fighter plane, a red space rocket. And my unmistakable childhood frown. Ringing and clanging the bell. The boat ride's OK. At least the water makes the air feel a little cool, cooler than this damn polyester turtleneck with the short sleeves. Circles . . . Grandma-Grandpa-Mom-Auntie Helen . . . Every eight seconds or so. All in polyester. Just like me.—Kami Lyle

Polyester, eeww, between my fingers, as I walk slowly down each ladies blouse aisle at the thrift shop. A gripping of each sleeve that's an attractive color to me, and a quick rub of the fabric between my fingers tells me whether if I want to get any closer to it. Most of the polyester I can tell just by looking at it and I don't even want to touch it. I can't believe how much of it there is around and that people really like to wear it. My skin protests in it. My mom clothed me in it almost completely for as long as she could. It's easy to take care of—doesn't require ironing. I'd itch and perspire and really stink in it—it doesn't breathe, so your skin can't either. And it's slippery and a petroleum product. It gives me an icky sad kind of feeling, as I'm thrift shopping, searching for silk blouses that women seem to be fairly happy to part with, because they think they have to dry-clean them. Nay, nay, you sillies. But you know, they're doing a good job with polyester blouses these days—some of them feel pretty close to silk.—Lynn Biddick

Polyester—Double knit thick choking stretch over fat—men and women's thighs, hips, and butts. Plastic shine that beams off their clothes especially under neon lights in shopping malls. Polyester un-real man-made even smells plastic when new. So what if it's easy to care for—it looks like shit. For some reason Indians (from India) love polyester. I'll see Indian couples—the women wearing the saris which I assume are all natural fibers—but the men have on those polyester plaid (or if no design, are an old ugly plain brownish tan) slacks on. Slacks somehow a fitting word when discussing polyester. A high school friend told me her father (an Indian) loved polyester "they are so comfortable!" was his excuse. Sarah was also a traditional Indian dancer. She was quite incredible to watch. Her hands over her head framing it in a diamond, while she would move her neck up, down, backward, forward, round and round as if it were not connected at all to the rest of her body. Feet stomping, legs lifting, arms waving in contorted positions that seemed impossible to be done. She would dance as if possessed by the music. I went to a few shows and watched in amazement at the human body's agility when put to the test. But back to polyester. Sarah hated going to these shows she gave because as she put it, "Indians don't know how to dress—I don't know why but they all wear that tacky and gross polyester double knit."—Eve Goodman

I see a secondhand suit—orange, or baby blue, or baby-shit brown. Or white, with a collar so wide it looks like it could fly. A miracle fabric of impracticality. It traps every bodily odor, binds every particle of dirt, but shows nothing. But it's all in there. I know it is, because nobody washes polyester. Can't picture it wet. Does it absorb water or repel it? Dacron suit, flared at hip and hem. Boldly stitched on the pockets. Some old man's Kleenex in here, like an old hair ball, or cocoon. God, what's in the breast pocket? I'm not sticking my finger in there. The lining is like a parachute, like a wind breaker. Why on

the inside, tho'? This is unnatural. The slacks—the long zipper starts in the nether regions of the crotch—in the bottom land—this man must have worn his waist band up around his ribs. He was perhaps one of those pear-shaped men who look like they might be concealing a uterus in their rather feminine abdomen. The legs are bell bottoms. Double knit. Thick. Sticks to my fingers. No good to caress. And you would not gratefully accept this coat on a cold night and clutch it around your formal shoulders. And you wouldn't slyly slip your hand under the starched restaurant table cloth to find the knee wearing these pants. And yet this was some man's suit. His go-to-meeting clothes. Maybe his Sunday best. His Christmas Day jacket. I am sad. I see the formal wear rack at Sears. He probably wanted something better. Don't we all. I keep seeing a black man in an Oldsmobile with cheap leather shoes and shiny gold buckles. I don't know why.
—Gillian Welch

Blue dotted suit in apartment rental office—cigarette butts in the tin ashtray; M&M's in the paper clip box—five phones, quiet as snow at midnight—Christmas lights sparkle—glitter in my cat's eye. Curled in his box—pink towel wrapped cushion—heater blaring heat—frosty windows. Still night. Trees crying outside, lamplight glowing. Laundry basket tipping over with socks—hockey socks, locker room, kilts and cleats—goalie padded down—Styrofoam egg carton toy in second grade: "Let's make a centipede!" Legs run around your neck like jellyfish. Tickle tickle, you make me giggle. Soda pop bubbles, here's a peanut butter cracker. Birds pecking at the plastic disc, birds on the wire—crows flying over the neighbor's house, warning, black. Soot. Fireplace warm, rug braided like autumn hair— braids of bread—Challah. Wine and grapes, purple dots, purple stems, caught in my brain.—Renee Margaret

There. Your first group writing experience. Get some people together and try it. You'll enjoy the experience and the company.

If you write on computer, create a file for your gems. When an exciting image or idea drops in to your Object Writing, mark it and save it in your file (Mine is called *frag.*) If you write in a notebook, leave the first five pages blank and transfer the gems there. The gem spot will be a good place to look for interesting stuff when you need stimulation.

Though Object Writing generates nifty lyric ideas, the main purpose is stimulation, deepening the world you swim in. Over the weeks and months your senses will take you places you never would have been, as you see the world more and more through your writer's eyes.

Object Writing makes the art of diving automatic, a sensible habit. Even when you start exploring abstractions like "friendship," you'll dive instinctively where the good stuff is—into your own unique sense pool, rather than into some ether of abstractions. Your lyric writing will benefit by drawing from a unique and provocative source, and everyone will listen. I promise.

Chapter Two

Making Metaphors

etaphors are not user-friendly. They are hard to find and hard to use well. Unfortunately, metaphor is a mainstay of good lyric writing; indeed, of most creative writing. From total snores like "break my heart" and "feel the emptiness inside" to awakening shocks like "the arc of a love affair" (Paul Simon), "feather canyons" (Joni Mitchell), "soul with no leak at the seam"(Peter Gabriel), and "Brut and charisma poured from the shadows" (Steely Dan), metaphors support lyrics like bone. The trick is to know how to build them.

In its most basic form, metaphor is a collision between ideas that don't belong together. It jams them together and leaves us to struggle with the consequences: for example, an *army* is a *rabid wolf*.

We watch the soldiers begin to snarl, grow snouts and foam at the teeth. The army disappears and we are left to face something red-eyed and dangerous. Of course, an army isn't a wolf. All metaphors must be literally false. If the things we identify are the same, e.g., a house is a dwelling place, there is no metaphor, only definition. Conflict is essential for metaphor. Put things that don't belong together in the same room, and watch the friction: *dog* with *wind*; *torture* with *car*; *cloud* with *river*.

Interesting overtones. Let's look closer. There are three types of metaphor:

- **Expressed Identity**—asserts an identity between two nouns, e.g., fear is a shadow; a cloud is a sailing ship. Expressed identity comes in three forms:

"x is y" (fear is a shadow)
"the y of x" (the shadow of fear)
"x's y" (fear's shadow)

Run each of these through all three forms:

wind = yelping dog
wind = river
wind = highway

Now come up with a few of your own and run them through all three forms. You might even extend them into longer versions, e.g., clouds are sailing ships on rivers of wind.

⊙ **Qualifying Metaphor**—Adjectives qualify nouns; adverbs qualify verbs. Friction within these relationships creates metaphor, e.g., hasty clouds; to sing blindly.

◢ **Verbal Metaphor**—formed by conflict between the verb and its subject and/or object, e.g., clouds sail; he tortured his clutch; frost gobbles summer down.

Aristotle says that the ability to see one thing as another is the only truly creative human act. Most of us have the creative spark to make metaphors, we just need to train and direct our energy properly. Look at this metaphor from Shelley's *Ode to the West Wind*: "A heavy *weight of hours* has chained and bowed/One too like thee . . ."

Hours are links of a chain, accumulating weight and bending the old man's back lower and lower as each new hour is added. An interesting way to look at old age . . .

Great metaphors seem to come in a flare of inspiration—there is a moment of light and heat, and suddenly the writer sees the old man bent over, dragging a load of invisible hour-chains. But even if great metaphors come from inspiration, you can certainly prepare yourself for their flaring. Here are some exercises to train your vision; to help you learn to look in the hot places; to help you nurture a spark that can erupt into something bright and wonderful.

PLAYING IN KEYS

Like musical notes, words can group together in close relationships, like belonging to the same key. Call this a *diatonic* relationship. For example, here are some random words that are diatonic to (in the same key as) tide: ocean; moon; recede; power; beach.

This is "playing in the key of *tide*," where *tide* is the fundamental tone. This is a way of creating collisions between elements that have at least some things in common—a fertile ground for metaphor. There are many other keys "tide" can belong to when something else is a fundamental tone, for example, power. Let's play in its key: Muhammad Ali; avalanche; army; Wheaties; socket; tide.

All these words are related to each other by virtue of their relationship to "power." If we combine them into little collisions we can often discover metaphors:

Muhammad Ali avalanched over his opponents.
An avalanche is an army of snow.
This army is the Wheaties of our revolution.
Wheaties plug your morning into a socket.
A socket holds back tides of electricity.

Try playing in the key of moon: stars; harvest; lovers; crescent; astronauts; calendar; tide.

The New Mexico sky is a rich harvest of stars.
Evening brings a harvest of lovers to the beach.
The lovers' feelings waned to a mere crescent.
The crescent of human knowledge grows with each astronaut's mission.
Astronauts' flights are a calendar of human courage.
A new calendar washes in a tide of opportunities.

Essentially, metaphor works by revealing some third thing that two ideas share in common. One good way of finding metaphors is by asking these two questions:

1. What characteristics does my idea ("tide") have?
2. What else has those characteristics?

Answering the second question usually releases a flood of possible metaphors.

Often the relationship between two ideas is not clear. "Muhammad Ali" is hardly the first idea that comes to mind with "avalanche," unless you recognize their linking term, "power." In most contexts, "Muhammad Ali" and "avalanche" are non-diatonic, unrelated to each other. Only when you look to find a link do you come up with "power," or "deadly," or "try to keep quiet when you're in their territories." Asking the two questions above opens up these relationships and helps you develop metaphor-seeking habits. Here are several exercises to help you get hooked.

EXERCISE

Get a group together, at least four people. Divide the participants into two equal groups. Each member of group one makes an arbitrary list of five interesting adjectives. At the same time, each member of group two makes an arbitrary list of five interesting nouns. Then their arbitrary lists are combined, usually resulting in some pretty strange combinations. For example,

adjectives	nouns
smoky	conversation
refried	railroad
decaffeinated	rainbow
hollow	rain forest
understated	eyebrows

Think about each combination for a minute. They evoke some interesting possibilities. Take any combination and try to write a sentence or short paragraph from it. Like this: "Since I got your phone call, everything seems dull. My day has been bleached of sound and color. Even the rainbow this afternoon has been decaffeinated."

EXERCISE

Try writing a sentence or short paragraph for these combinations:

smoky conversation
refried railroad
hollow rain forest
understated eyebrows

Now jumble them up into different combinations (for example, *smoky eyebrows*) and write a sentence or short paragraph for each one. The point of the exercise is to see what overtones (linking ideas, metaphors) are released by this blind striking of notes.

Wonderful accidents happen frequently.

EXERCISE

Each member of group one makes an arbitrary list of five interest-ing verbs. At the same time, each member of group two makes an arbitrary list of five interesting nouns. Like these:

nouns	verbs
squirrel	preaches
wood stove	vomits
surfboard	cancels
reef	celebrates
aroma	palpitates

Again, take any combination and try to write a sentence or short paragraph from it. Like this: "The red squirrel scrambled onto the branch, rose to his haunches and began preaching to us, apparently cautioning us to respect the silence of his woodlands."
Your turn.

wood stove vomits
surfboard cancels
reef celebrates
aroma palpitates

Jumbling up the list unveils new combinations. Write a sen-tence or short paragraph for each one:

nouns	verbs
squirrel	celebrates
wood stove	palpitates
surfboard	preaches
reef	cancels
aroma	vomits

If you don't already have a writers' group, these exercises might be a good reason to start one. Just get some people together (even numbers are best) and start making arbitrary lists. Put your lists together and see what your combinations suggest.

One thing becomes clear right away: you get better results combining nouns and verbs than from combining adjectives and nouns. Verbs are the power amplifiers of language. They drive it; set it in motion. Look at any of the great poets—e.g., Yeats, Frost, Sexton, Eliot. If you actually go through some poems and circle their verbs, you will see why the poems crackle with power. Great writers know where to look. They pay attention to their verbs.

EXERCISE

Each member of group one makes an arbitrary list of five interesting nouns. At the same time, each member of group two also makes an arbitrary list of five interesting nouns. Like these:

nouns	nouns
summer	Rolls-Royce
ocean	savings account
thesaurus	paintbrush
Indian	beach ball
shipwreck	mattress

Remember the three forms of expressed identity, the first type of metaphor? Try these noun-noun collisions in each form. For example,

Summer is a Rolls-Royce
the Rolls-Royce of summer
summer's Rolls-Royce

Summer is the Rolls-Royce of the seasons.
Winter is gone. Time for another ride in the Rolls-Royce of summer.
Once again, summer's Rolls-Royce has collapsed into the iceboat of winter.

Your turn again. Use whatever form of expressed identity seems to work best. Write a sentence or short paragraph for the other four.

Of course, these are great fun to jumble up. You can even jumble them within the same columns. Try a sentence for each of these:

nouns	nouns
summer	mattress
ocean	paintbrush
thesaurus	beach ball
Indian	Rolls-Royce
shipwreck	savings account

EXERCISE

After you have spent a few sessions discovering accidental metaphors through the previous exercises, you will be ready for the final method to activate the process: a five-step exercise guaranteed to open your metaphorical eyes and keep them open.

Step One: Make a list of five interesting adjectives. Then, for each one, find an interesting noun that creates a fresh, exciting metaphor. Take as long as you need for each adjective—hours, even days. Keep it in your vision. Push it against every noun you see until you create a breathtaking collision. Be patient. Developing a habit of looking takes time. It is the quality of your metaphors and the accumulated hours of practice that count here, not speed.

Remember that you can make vivid adjectives out of verbs: *to wrinkle* becomes the adjective *wrinkled (wrinkled water)* or *wrinkling (the wrinkling hours.)* These are called participles. Remember?

Step Two: Now make a list of five interesting nouns, and locate a terrific verb for each one. This will be harder, since you are used to looking at things in the world, not actions. Again, take your time. Develop a habit of mind that can see a doe stepping through the shallows as the water *wrinkles* into circles around her.

Step Three: Make a list of five interesting verbs and track down a noun for each one. Most likely, you've never looked at the world from this angle before. You'll find it unnatural, challenging and fun.

Step Four: Make a list of five interesting nouns and find an adjective for each one. (Don't forget about participles.)

Step Five: Make a list of five interesting nouns and find another noun for each one. Use whatever form of expressed identity you think works best.

This last step brings you full circle. You have looked at the world from the vantage point of nouns, verbs and adjectives. (I left out adverbs as a matter of personal preference. I don't get much use out of them, especially when I am careful to find strong verbs. If you want to add them to the exercise, simply list five adverbs and find a verb for each one. Then reverse the process and start with a list of verbs.) This is a practical result: Because you have developed a *habit of looking*, you will see countless opportunities to create metaphors in your writing. After all, you run into nouns, verbs and adjectives pretty frequently . . .

These exercises focus your creative attention on a practical way to find metaphors using expressed identity, qualifying metaphors and verbal metaphors. You don't have to wait for a grand bolt of inspiration. Simply look at the word you're on, and ask,

1. What characteristics does this idea have?
2. What else has those characteristics?

Then watch ideas tumble out onto your page.

SIMILE

You learned in high school that the difference between metaphor and simile is that simile uses *like* or *as*. True enough, but that's like saying that measles are spots on your body. They are, but if you look deeper, the spots are there because a virus is present. There is something more fundamental going on. Remember the metaphor *an army is a rabid wolf*? Say it to yourself and let the pictures roll. You start with army but your focus transfers to the rabid wolf, something red-eyed and dangerous.

Simile doesn't transfer focus: an army is *like* a rabid wolf. Say it to yourself and let the pictures roll. The army refuses to budge. No snouts or foamy teeth. We sit waiting for an explanation while the army stands before us in full uniform.

Look at this from Kurt Thompson:

> My love is an engine
> It ain't run in years
> Just took one kiss from you
> to loosen up the gears

My heart needs to rev some
It's an old Chevrolet
You might think it's crazy
To want to race away

Who ever said
that love was smart

Baby won't you drive my heart
Won't you drive my heart

The metaphor sets up the car. The speaker is asking *Baby* to get in and step on the accelerator. Now look at this version:

My love's **like** an engine
It ain't run in years
Just took one kiss from you
to loosen up these gears

My heart needs to rev some
Like an old Chevrolet
You might think it's crazy
To want to race away

Who ever said
that love was smart

Baby won't you drive my heart
Won't you drive my heart

Read it again and let the pictures roll. Now the focus stays on the speaker rather than transferring to the car. So the emphasis in "Baby won't you drive my heart" is on heart rather than drive. It seems like a subtle difference, but it makes all the difference in how we hear the song. The metaphor creates a light, clever song. The simile is clever too, but more intimate, since we stay in the presence of the speaker throughout the song.

Because simile refuses to transfer focus, it works in a totally different way than metaphor. Metaphor takes its second term (an army is a *rabid dog*) very seriously—you must commit to it, because that's what everyone will end up looking at.

You needn't commit as deeply to the second term of the simile, since the first term gets most of the attention. This makes simile useful as a one-time event. In *I'm as corny as Kansas in August*, our focus stays on *I*. We have no further appetite for corn or Kansas. Good thing, since the rest of the song goes everywhere but Kansas. However, if the line had been "I am corn in Kansas in August," we'd expect to hear things about sun, rain, wind and harvest in the upcoming lines.

As a rule of thumb, when you have several comparisons in mind, use simile:

> Love is like rain
> Love is like planting
> Love is like the summer sun

When you're using only one, e.g., *Love is a rose*, and you want to commit to it throughout the song, use metaphor. It only grows when it's on the vine.

Chapter Three

Learning to Say No
Building Worksheets

Writing a lyric is like getting a gig: if you're grateful for any idea that comes along, you're probably not getting the best stuff. But if you have lots of legitimate choices, you won't end up playing six hours in Bangor Maine for twenty bucks. Look at it this way: the more often you can say no, the better your gigs get. That's why I suggest that you learn to build a worksheet—a specialized tool for brainstorming that produces bathtubs full of ideas and, at the same time, tailors the ideas specifically for a lyric.

Simply, a worksheet contains two things: a list of key ideas, and a list of rhymes for each one. There are three stages to building a worksheet.

1. FOCUS YOUR LYRIC IDEA AS CLEARLY AS YOU CAN

Let's say you want to write about homelessness. Sometimes you'll start the lyric from an emotion: "That old homeless woman with everything she owns in a shopping cart really touches me. I want to write a song about her." Sometimes you'll write from a cold, calculated idea: "I'm tired of writing love songs. I want to do one on a serious subject, maybe homelessness." Or, you may write from a title you like, maybe, *Risky Business*. Then the trick is to find an interesting angle on it, perhaps: "What do you do for a living?" "I survive on the streets." "That's a pretty Risky Business."

In each case, it's up to you to find the angle, brainstorm the idea, and create the world the idea will live in. Since you always bring your unique perspective to each experience, you will have something interesting to offer. But you'll have to look at enough ideas to find the best perspective.

Object Writing is the key to developing choices. You must dive into your vaults of sense material—those unique and secret places—to find out what images you've stored away, in the present example, around the idea of homelessness.

STOP Stop reading, get out a pen and dive into homelessness for ten minutes. Stay *sense-bound and very specific*. How do you connect to the idea? Did you ever get lost in the woods as a child? Run away from home? Sleep in a car in New York?

Now, did you find an expressive image, like a broken wheel on her shopping cart, that can serve as a metaphor—a vehicle to carry your feelings? Did you see some situation, like your parents fighting, that seems to connect you with her situation? These expressive objects or situations are what T.S. Eliot calls "objective correlatives"—*objects* anyone can touch, smell, see that *correlate* with the emotion you want to express. Broken wheels or parents fighting work nicely as objective correlatives.

Even if you find ideas that work well, keep looking a while longer. When you find a good idea, there is usually a bunch behind it. (The gig opening for Aerosmith could be the next offer.) Jot down your good ideas on a separate sheet.

2. MAKE A LIST OF WORDS THAT EXPRESS YOUR IDEA

You'll need to look further than the hot ideas from your Object Writing. Get out a thesaurus, one set up according to Roget's original plan according to the flow of ideas—a setup perfect for brainstorming. Dictionary-style versions (set up alphabetically) are useful only for finding synonyms and antonyms. They make brainstorming a cumbersome exercise in cross-referencing.

Your thesaurus is better than a good booking agent. It can churn up images and ideas you wouldn't ever get to by yourself, stimulating your diver to greater and greater depths until choices to say no to litter the beaches.

Let's adopt the working title *Risky Business* and continue brainstorming the idea of homelessness. In the index (the last half of your thesaurus) locate a word that expresses the general idea, for example, "risk." From the list below it, select the word most related to the lyric idea. My thesaurus lists these: risk: gambling 618n; possibility 469n; danger 661n; speculate 791vb. Read the first notation as follows: "you will find the word *risk* in the noun group of section 618 under the key word *gambling*."

Key words are always in *italics*. They set a general meaning for the section, like a key signature sets the tone center in a piece of music.

Probably the closest meaning for our purposes with *Risky Business* is *danger* 661n. Look in the text (front half) of the thesaurus for section 661. (Or whatever number your thesaurus lists. Numbers will appear at the tops of the pages.) If you peruse the general area around *danger* for a minute, you will find several pages of related material. Here are the surrounding section headings:

Ill health, disease;	Insalubrity	Deterioration
Relapse	Bane	Danger
Pitfall	Danger signal	Escape
Salubrity (well-being);	Improvement	Restoration
Remedy	Safety	Refuge. Safeguard
Warning	Preservation	Deliverance

This related material runs for 16 pages in double column entries. *Risk* is totally surrounded by its relatives, so if you look around the neighborhood, you'll find a plethora of possibilities. Start building your list.

Look at these first few entries under *danger*: N. *danger*, peril; . . . shadow of death, jaws of d., dragon's mouth, dangerous situation, unhealthy s., desperate s., forlorn hope 700n. *predicament*; emergency 137n. *crisis*; insecurity, jeopardy, risk, hazard, ticklishness . . .

Look actively. If you take each entry for a quick dive through your sense memories, you should have a host of new ideas within minutes. (Frequent Object Writing pays big dividends here: the more familiar you are with the process, the quicker these quick dives get. If you are slow at first, don't give up—you'll get faster. Just vow to do more Object Writing.) Jot down the best words on your list and keep at it until you're into serious overload.

Now the fun begins. Start saying no to words in your list until you've trimmed it to about ten or twelve words with different vowel sounds in their stressed syllables. Put these survivors in the middle of a blank sheet of paper, number them, and enclose them in a box for easy reference later on. Keep these guidelines in mind:

1. If you are working with a title, be sure to put its key vowel sounds in the list.
2. Most of your words should end in a stressed syllable, since they work best in rhyming position.
3. Put interesting words that duplicate a vowel sound in parentheses.

Your goal is to create a list of words to look up in your rhyming dictionary.

Here's what I got banging around in the thesaurus, looking through the lens of homelessness:

1. risk
2. business
3. left out
4. freeze (wheel, shield)
5. storm
6. dull (numb)
7. night (child)
8. change
9. defense
10. home (hope, broken, coat)

This is not a final list. Don't be afraid to switch, add, or take words out as the process continues.

3. LOOK UP EACH WORD IN YOUR RHYMING DICTIONARY

Be sure to extend your search to imperfect rhyme types, and to select only words that connect with your ideas. Above all, don't bother with cliché rhymes or other typical rhymes. First, a quick survey of rhyme types.

Perfect Rhyme

Don't be seduced by the word "perfect." It doesn't mean "better," it only means:

1. The syllables' vowel sounds are the same.
2. The consonant sounds after the vowels (if any) are the same.
3. The sounds before the vowels are different.

Remember, lyrics are sung, not read or spoken. When you sing, you exaggerate vowels. And since rhyme is a vowel connection, lyricists can make sonic connections in ways other than perfect rhyme. Here are the most useful:

Family Rhyme

1. The syllables' vowel sounds are the same.
2. The consonant sounds after the vowels belong to the same phonetic families.
3. The sounds before the vowels are different.

Here's a chart of the three important consonant families:

	PLOSIVES	FRICATIVES	NASALS
Voiced:	b d g	v TH z zh j	m n ng
Unvoiced:	p t k	f th s sh ch	

Each of the three boxes, plosives, fricatives and nasals, form a phonetic family. When a word ends in a consonant in one of the boxes, you can use the other members of the family to find perfect rhyme substitutes.

Rub/up/thud/putt/bug/stuck are members of the same family—plosives, so they are family rhymes.

Love/buzz/judge/fluff/fuss/hush/touch are members of the fricative family, so they rhyme. *Strum/run/sung* rhyme as members of the nasal family.

Say you want to rhyme line two, below:

> Tire tracks across my face
> I'm stuck in a rut

First, look up perfect rhymes for *rut*: cut, glut, gut, hut, shut.

The trick to saying something you mean is to expand your alternatives. Look at the Table of Family Rhymes and introduce yourself to t's relatives.

ud	uk	ub	up	ug
blood	buck	club	hard up	bug
flood	duck	hub	makeup	jug
mud	luck	pub	cup	unplug
stud	muck	scrub		plug
thud	stuck	tub		shrug
	truck			snug
				tug

Much better. That's a lot of interesting stuff to say no to. Now, how about this:

> Tire tracks across my back
> There's nowhere I feel safe

First, look up perfect rhymes for *safe* in your rhyming dictionary. All we get is *waif*. Not much. Now look for family rhymes under f's family, the *fricatives*: We add these possibilities:

as	av	az	aj
case	behave	blaze	age
ace	brave	craze	cage
breathing-	cave	daze	page
space	grave	haze	rage
chase	shave	phrase	stage
face	slave	paraphrase	
disgrace	wave	praise	**aTH**
embrace			bathe
grace	**ath**		
lace	faith		
resting-place			
space			

Finally, nasals. The word "nasals" means what you think it means: all the sound comes out of your nose.

> Tire tracks across my head
> Pounding like a drum

Look up perfect rhymes for *drum*: hum; pendulum; numb; slum; strum.

Go to the Table of Family Rhymes and introduce yourself to m's relatives:

un	**ung**
fun	hung
gun	flung
overrun	wrung
won	sung
jettison	
skeleton	

Finding family rhyme isn't hard, and its rewards are amazing. So there's no reason to tie yourself in knots using only perfect rhyme when family rhyme sounds so close. When sung, the ear won't know the difference.

Additive Rhyme

1. The syllables' vowel sounds are the same.
2. One of the syllables adds extra consonants after the vowel.
3. The sounds before the vowels are different.

When the syllable you want to rhyme ends in a vowel, e.g., play, free, fly, the only way to generate alternatives is to add consonants after the vowel. The guideline is simple: The less sound you add, the closer you stay to perfect rhyme.

Look again at the Table of Family Rhymes. Voiced plosives, *b*, *d*, *g*, put out the least sound. Use them first, rhyming, for example, *ricochet* with *paid*. then the unvoiced plosives, rhyming *free* with e.g., *treat*. Next voiced fricatives, rhyming *fly* and e.g., *alive*. Then on to unvoiced fricatives, followed finally by the most noticeable consonants (aside from *l* and *r*), the nasals. You'd end up with a list moving from closest to perfect rhyme to farthest away: *free*: speed; cheap; sweet; grieve; belief; dream; clean; deal.

Of course you can add consonants even if there are already consonants after the vowel. For example, street/sweets, alive/drives, dream/screamed, trick/risk.

You can even combine this technique with family rhyme, e.g., dream/cleaned, club/floods/shove/stuffed. This gives you even more options, making it easier to say what you mean.

Subtractive Rhyme

1. The syllables' vowel sounds are the same.
2. One of the syllables adds an extra consonant after the vowel.
3. The sounds before the vowels are different.

It's basically the same as additive rhyme. The difference is practical. If you start with *fast, class* is subtractive. If you start with *class, fast* is additive.

> Tire tracks across my face
> Help, I'm sinking fast

fast: glass; flat; mashed (family); laughed (family); crash (fam. subt.)
The possibilities grow.

Assonance Rhyme

1. The syllables' vowel sounds are the same.
2. The consonant sounds after the vowels are unrelated.
3. The sounds before the vowels are different.

This is the farthest you can get from perfect rhyme without changing vowel sounds. Consonants after the vowels have nothing in common. Check these out:

> Tire tracks across my face
> I hope you're satisfied

satisfied: life; trial; crime; sign; rise; survive; surprise
Use these techniques. You'll have much more leeway saying what you mean, and your rhymes will be fresh and useful. Again, look actively at each word. Dive through your senses with them as though you were Object Writing.

Brainstorming with a rhyming dictionary prepares you to write a *lyric*. At the same time you are brainstorming your ideas, you are also finding sounds you can use later. With solid rhyming techniques that include family rhymes, additive and subtractive rhymes, assonance and even consonance rhymes (especially for "l" and "r"), using a rhyming dictionary can be as relaxed and easy as brainstorming with a friend, except it's more efficient than a friend and it won't whine for a piece of the song if you get a hit.

Here is a sample worksheet including both perfect and imperfect rhymes.

A worksheet externalizes the inward process of lyric writing. It slows your writing process down so you can get to know it better, like slowing down when you play a new scale to help get it under your fingers. The more you do it, the faster and more efficient you'll get.

Reading this worksheet should be stimulating. But doing your own worksheet will set you on fire. Decide now that you will do a complete worksheet for each of your next ten lyrics, then stick to it. The first one will be slow and painful, but full of new and interesting options. By the third one, ideas will be coming fast and furious. You will have too much to say, too many choices, and too many rhymes. Though getting to this point takes work, it will be well worth the effort. Think of all the times you'll get to say no. No more clichés. No more forced rhymes. No more helpless gratitude that some idea, any idea at all came along. No more six-hour gigs in Bangor for twenty bucks. Trust me.

WORKSHEET:
Risky Business

1. risk
2. business
3. left out
4. freeze (wheel, shield)
5. storm
6. dull (numb)
7. night (child)
8. change
9. defense
10. home (hope, broken, coat)

1. risk
cliff
fist
kissed
stiff
itch
pitch
drift
switch
shift
pinched
chips

2. business
collisions
visions
frigid
forgiveness
submissive
delicious
riches
suspicious
kisses
finish
wind

3. left out
proud
bound
count
vowed
aloud
renowned
aroused
crowned

4. freeze
grieve
leave
peace
appeased
street
debris
diseased
guarantee(s)
wheel
shield

5. storm
reform
(re)born
court
cord
scorn
divorce
reward
warm
torn
ignored

6. dull
sulk
annulled
cult
pale
brawl
numb
opium
martyrdom
crumbs
gun
young

7. night
flight
spite
bride
strike
prize
despised
deprived
child
fault
crawl

8. change
cage
slave
grave
safe
faith
castaway
ricochet
haste

9. defense
expense
bench
trench
drenched
friend
revenge
content
condemned
contempt

10. home
disowned
blown
bone
unknown
stoned
dethroned
zone
hope
coat
throat
remote
ghost
Job
load
broken

Chapter Four

Clichés:
The Sleeping Puppy
(A Case Study)

♪ ♪ ♪

T he PBS documentary scene: a black puppy scampers across the lawn chasing a butterfly when, plop, she drops limp on her side, fast asleep. Moments later she's up and romping. Then again, plop. "Narcolepsy," intones the narrator, "can strike its victim at any time. She'll sleep a few minutes then get up and move on, unaware that anything happened. Scientists cite a variety of possible causes."

The documentary fails to mention the radio playing in the background. Watch and listen closely—the puppy topples over at the lines "You gotta take a chance / If you want a true romance." She sleeps until the song finishes, then gets up chasing her tail until she hears "Take my hand/ Let me know you understand." Plop. I may not be the *New England Journal of Medicine,* but I know why the puppy is falling asleep: clichés. Cliché phrases. Cliché rhymes. Cliché images. Cliché metaphors. These viruses infect songs, television, movies, and commercials, not to mention everyday conversations. And if clichés can put puppies to sleep, think what they'll do to people who listen to your songs.

Clichés have been worn smooth by overuse. They no longer mean what they used to. *Strong as a bull, eats like a horse, their ship came in,* no longer evoke vivid images of bulls, horses and ships. Overuse has made them generic. They suffer from the same malady that infects all generic language: they don't show—they can only tell. *How ya doin'? What's up? How's it goin'?* are interchangeable. So are *Break my heart. Cut me deep. Hurt me bad.* Your job as a writer isn't to point to a generic territory where images could be, but to go there, get one, and *show* it to your listeners. Clichés don't pump gasoline anymore.

Songs should be universal, but don't mistake universal for generic. Sense-bound is universal. When you stimulate your listeners' senses, they pick pictures from their own personal sense files. When you use generic language, they fall asleep. There's a difference between this,

> 1. . Noise and confusion, there's no peace
>   In the hustle and bustle of city streets
>   It's time to get away from it all
>   Deep inside I hear nature's call

and this from Yeats:

> 2. I will arise and go now . . .
>   I hear lake water lapping with low sounds by the shore
>   While I stand on the roadway, or the pavements gray,
>   I hear it in the deep heart's core.

Both express roughly the same sentiment, but the first, cliché and generic as it is, can only point to territories of meaning. Yeats takes you there.

Clichés are prefabricated. You can string them together as easily as a guitarist strings his favorite licks into a solo. (two Claptons + one Hendrix + three Pages + one Stevie Ray . . . etc.) The problem is, it isn't *his* solo. Using other peoples' licks is an excellent way to learn, but there is a next step—finding your own way of saying it. Clichés are other peoples' licks. They don't come from *your* emotions.

Look at the sample lists of clichés below. They're all familiar—maybe uncomfortably familiar.

Cliché Phrases

(way down) deep inside	touch my (very) soul	take my hand
hand in-hand	heart-to-heart	eye to eye
face-to-face	side by side	in and out
back and forth	up and down	by my side
walk out (that) door	we've just begun	hurts so bad
feel the pain	can't stand the pain	can't take it
gotta take a chance	give me half a chance	last chance
	such a long time	night and day

take your time
the rest of time
end of time
no one like you
say you'll be mine
how it used to be
it's gonna be all right
set me free
work it out
true to you
kiss your lips
falling apart
taken for granted
lost without you
safe and warm
broken heart
all we've been through
end of the line
always be true
pay the price
right or wrong
what we're fighting for
you know it's true
hold me close
forget my foolish pride
drive me crazy
all my dreams come
    true

all night long
rest of my life
no one can take your
    place
losing sleep
made up my mind
get down on my knees
end it all
had your fun
done you wrong
back to me
make you stay
asking too much
no tomorrow
give you my heart
aching heart
want you/need you/
    love you
hold on
never let you (me) go
rise above
all we've done
worth fighting for
nothing to lose
losing sleep
treat me like a fool
going insane
rhyme or reason

the test of time
someone like you
all my love
lonely nights
I'll get along
calling out your name
more than friends
fooling around
heaven above
break these chains
take it easy
can't live without you
somebody else
break my heart
try one more time
can't go on
keep holding on
now or never
over the hill
know for sure
hold me tight
tear me apart
play the game
see the light
O baby

Clichés come effortlessly. It's no sweat to string them together and feel like you've said something.

> She sits alone all day long
> The hours pass her by
> Every minute like the last
> A prisoner of time

It does say something, just nothing startling. It doesn't yank you by the hair into her room. No humming fluorescent lights. No faded lace curtains. You get to nap securely at a distance, untouched, uninvolved. Getting to the good stuff is harder work. Though clichés are great in a first or second draft as *place markers* for something better, don't ever mistake them for the real thing.

She's wheeled into the hallway
Till the sun moves down the floor
Little squares of daylight
Like a hundred times before

CLICHÉ RHYMES

When you hear one of these, no need to lose sleep wondering what's coming next. Plop. Nap time.

---

hand/understand/command
walk/talk
kiss/miss
dance/chance/romance
friend/end
cry/die/try/lie/good-bye/deny
best/rest/test
love/above/dove
hide/inside/denied
touch/much
begun/done
blues/lose
lover/discover/cover
light/night/sight/tight/fight/right
take it/make it/fake it/shake it
change/rearrange
stronger/longer

eyes/realize/sighs/lies
fire/desire/higher
burn/yearn/learn
forever/together/never
ache/break
tears/fears
door/before/more
heart/start/apart/part
wrong/strong/song/long
word/heard
arms/charms/harm/warm
true/blue/through
pain/rain/same
touch/much
maybe/baby
knees/please

Most cliché rhymes are perfect rhymes, a good reason to stretch into other rhyme types—family rhyme, additive and subtractive rhyme, and even assonance rhyme. These imperfect rhyme types are guaranteed fresh, and most listeners won't notice the difference.

CLICHÉ IMAGES

These have been aired out so much they are mere whiffs of their former selves:

---

lips	eyes	smile	hands
face	hair	silky hair	voice
soft (smooth)	warmth of arms	kiss	moon
skin	sky	light	sun going down

stars	shadow	bed	lying in bed
night	crying	knock	door
tears	key	door	wall
lock	chains	flowers	rose
cuts like a knife	glass of wine	fireplace	telephone
perfume	feel the beat	sweat	flashing lights
dance floor			

The best cure for cliché images is to dive into your own sense pool and discover images that communicate *your* feelings. What did your lover say? Where were you? What kind of car? What was the texture of the upholstery in the back seat? . . . You get the idea.

CLICHÉ METAPHORS

Review chapter two, Making Metaphors. There's no reason to keep sleepwalking in these yellow fogs.

Storm for anger, including thunder, lightning, dark clouds, flashing, wind, hurricane, tornado etc.

Fire for love or passion, including burn, spark, heat, flame, too hot, consumed, burned, ashes.

Cold for emotional indifference, including ice, freeze, frozen etc.

Light for knowledge or happiness, including shine, sun, touch the sky, blinded by love, and others too numerous to mention.

Darkness for ignorance, sadness and loneliness, including night, blind, shadows, etc.

Rain for tears.

Seasons for stages of life or relationships.

Walls for protection from harm, especially from love.

Drown in love.

Broken heart.

Prison, Prisoner used especially for love, includes chains etc.

I've listed enough clichés to keep whole herds of puppies asleep for decades. If you have a barking dog in the neighborhood, instead of yelling try reading aloud from these lists in its general direction . . .

FRIENDLY CLICHÉS

In some cases, you can use a cliché to your advantage. Put it in a context that brings out its original meaning or makes us see it in a new way. For example, *I'll be seeing you*, as a cliché, is a substitute for *so long* or *good-bye*. When Sammy Fain and Irving

Kahal set it up, it's brand new:

> I'll be seeing you
> In all the old familiar places . . .
> I'll be looking at the moon
> But I'll be seeing you

It implies *good-bye,* but only as an overtone of the primary meaning. The result is a combination: after we say good-bye, I'll see you everywhere.

David Wilcox slants *it's all downhill from here* to his advantage in *Top of the Roller Coaster* with this setup:

> Say good-bye to your twenties
> Tomorrow is the big Three-O
> For your birthday present
> I've got a place where we can go
> It's a lesson in motion
> We'll ride the wildest ride
> We're going to climb to the top of the roller coaster
> And look down the other side
>
> Let me ride in the front car
> You ride right behind
> And I'll click my snapshot camera
> At exactly the right time
> I'll shoot back over my shoulder
> Catch the fear no one can hide
> When we tip the top of the roller coaster
> And look down the other side
> Over the hill
>
> So when the prints come back
> We can look at that unmistakable birthday fear
> Like your younger days are over now
> And it's all downhill from here

He also gets a new look at over-the-hill and tiptop while he's at it. Neat.

Without a terrific setup, duck whenever you see a cliché. They come easy and from all directions, so it's hard not to be infected. Your own senses and experiences are your best protection. So is brutal and resolute rewriting. I don't mean to sound revolutionary, but you might also try a diet of good literature and poetry. You are what you eat.

EXERCISE

For fun, try these two experiments: first, come up with your own lists of clichés, at least as long as mine. (It won't be hard.) Second, string some of yours and mine together into a verse-chorus-verse-chorus lyric, making sure nothing original sneaks in.

Knowledge brings responsibility. Now that you know the fundamental cause of puppy narcolepsy, you have a special responsibility to keep your writing sense-bound and original. No one likes a person who puts puppies to sleep.

Chapter Five

Verse Development

In its simplest form, this is the basic rule of songwriting: Keep your listeners interested all the way through your song. Get them with you from the beginning with a strong opening line, then keep them with you the rest of the way. Whether they stay or go is up to you.

Your verses are responsible for keeping listeners interested. They develop your idea; they are the basic tool to advance your concept, plot, or story. They get us ready to hear the chorus—they control the angle of entry and the way we see the chorus. Like parts of an essay, each one should focus on a separate idea.

Say we had a song whose only elements are verses, and the verse summaries went something like:

Verse 1. The sheriff is the toughest man in town.
Verse 2. He is very strong and has a fast gun.
Verse 3. Everyone in town knows the sheriff is tough. They are afraid of him.

The ideas don't move much. These verses say pretty much the same thing in different words. Obviously, they could be improved by more interesting language, images, or metaphors, but no matter how you polished the language, it would only disguise the fact that something important is missing.

The only real fix is to take the idea new places.

Verse 1. The sheriff is the toughest man in town.
Verse 2. He is obsessed with a beautiful woman.
Verse 3. She is married to the weakest man in town.

The language is still bland and imageless. Yet now we want to know what happens next. We had no such curiosity about the first sequence.

REPETITION

When you add a repeating section to the verses (a refrain or chorus), development is even more important. Stagnant verses turn repetition stagnant too. Watch.

Verse 1

The sheriff is the toughest man in town.
Beware, beware. All hands beware.

Verse 2

He is very strong and has a fast gun.
Beware, beware. All hands beware.

Verse 3

Everyone in town knows the sheriff is tough.
They are afraid of him.
Beware, beware. All hands beware.

The refrain suffers from the same disease as the verses—stagnation. Boredom is amplified. You can't fix stagnation by adding more, you have to change what's there. You have to develop the ideas.

Nor will it do to change the refrain every time. Then it isn't a refrain, but simply additional material. Remember, you don't fix stagnation by adding to it. You do the same thing you did when you had only verses—you develop the idea. Like this.

Verse 1

The sheriff is the toughest man in town.
Beware, beware. All hands beware.

Verse 2

He is obsessed with a beautiful woman.
Beware, beware. All hands beware.

Verse 3
> She is married to the weakest man in town.
> Beware, beware. All hands beware.

Now each refrain is a different color. It takes its color from what it attaches to. When it attaches to verses that mean the same thing, the refrain gets boring. When it attaches to verses that develop the idea, it dances.

Don't waste your verses. Don't let them sit idle waiting for the hook to come around and rescue them. Too often there won't be anyone around to witness the rescue.

PUT SEPARATE IDEAS IN SEPARATE SYSTEMS

Look at this lyric by Jon Jarvis and Gary Nicholson:

FATHERS AND SONS
My father had so much to tell me
Things he said I ought to know
Don't make my mistakes
There are rules you can't break
But I had to find out on my own

Now when I look at my own son
I know what my father went through
There's only so much you can do
You're proud when they walk
Scared when they run
That's how it always has been between FATHERS AND SONS

It's a bridge you can't cross
It's a cross you can't bear
It's the words you can't say
The things you can't change
No matter how much you care
So you do all you can
Then you've gotta let go
You're just part of the flow
Of the river that runs between FATHERS AND SONS

Your mother will try to protect you

Hold you as long as she can
But the higher you climb
The more you can see
That's something that I understand
One day you'll look at your own son
There'll be so much that you want to say
But he'll have to find his own way
On the road he must take
The course he must run
That's how it always has been between FATHERS AND SONS

It's a bridge you can't cross
It's a cross you can't bear
It's the words you can't say
The things you can't change
No matter how much you care
So you do all you can
Then you've gotta let go
You're just part of the flow
Of the river that runs between FATHERS AND SONS

What a nice lyric. For me, it really hits home, especially in the first chorus. It touches both the son and the father in me.

Fathers and Sons is made up of two large units, or *systems.* Verses one and two plus the first chorus make up system one. Verses three and four plus chorus two make the second system. Let's look at the first system.

My father had so much to tell me
Things he said I ought to know
Don't make my mistakes
There are rules you can't break
But I had to find out on my own

The speaker looks back at his father's attempts to help smooth the way ahead, and his own unwillingness to listen. Stubborn kid. Had to do it for himself when all that help was available.

Now when I look at my own son
I know what my father went through

> There's only so much you can do
> You're proud when they walk
> Scared when they run
> That's how it always has been between FATHERS AND SONS

Now the speaker is the father, going through the same things with his own son. He understands what he did to his father, but understands that it was necessary, perhaps even inevitable.

> That's how it always has been between FATHERS AND SONS

I love the structure of the verse: how it tosses in an extra line (line three), refuses to rhyme lines four and five, then extends the last line to focus our attention on the title. Lovely moves. Now the chorus:

> It's a bridge you can't cross
> It's a cross you can't bear
> It's the words you can't say
> The things you can't change
> No matter how much you care
> So you do all you can
> Then you've gotta let go
> You're just part of the flow
> Of the river that runs between FATHERS AND SONS

So far, very effective stuff. I've been interested the whole time. What a nifty chorus. I love the play on *cross:*

> It's a bridge you can't cross
> It's a cross you can't bear

and

> You're just part of the flow
> Of the river that runs between FATHERS AND SONS

The river is a divider of generations, but it's also the connector of generations. "Between" means "separation," but also means "from one to the other." The pattern repeats from father to son to father to son to father ... Neat word play. Both the message and the fancy dancing sweep me along. Now look at the second system:

> Your mother will try to protect you
> Hold you as long as she can
> But the higher you climb
> The more you can see
> That's something that I understand

This sounds familiar. Not that I've seen things from the mother's perspective yet, but I have seen the father, in fact both fathers, trying to protect the child. I've also seen the child trying to go beyond the parents. Not that this information isn't interesting, it's just not new. The ideas (if not the exact perspectives—*she* and *you*) have been covered. This doesn't bode well for the second chorus. We'll need development rather than restatement to keep repetition interesting.

> One day you'll look at your own son
> There'll be so much that you want to say
> But he'll have to find his own way
> On the road he must take
> The course he must run
> That's how it always has been between FATHERS AND SONS

Oops. I know I've been here before. It's verse two with *I* changed to *you*. No need to try to universalize verse four with "you." The idea was already universal. The second chorus is a goner. It can't help but say exactly the same thing as the first chorus.

> It's a bridge you can't cross
> It's a cross you can't bear
> It's the words you can't say
> The things you can't change
> No matter how much you care
> So you do all you can
> Then you've got let go
> You're just part of the flow

Of the river that runs between FATHERS AND SONS

It isn't so much that there is no advancement of the idea in verses three and four, there just isn't enough to give us a new look at the chorus when we get there. The power of this lovely chorus is diminished rather than enlarged the second time around, and we leave the song less interested than we were in the middle. Let's see if we can fix it.

The song contains two perspectives: a son looking at his father; and the son as father. If the first system could focus only on the son looking at his father, saying

> My father had so much to tell me
> Things he said I ought to know
> Don't make my mistakes
> There are rules you can't break
> But I had to find out on my own

> *V. 2 idea (in prose)*: "I kept him at arm's length.
> I didn't want him interfering with my life.
> He kept trying, but I wouldn't let him."
> That's how it always has been between FATHERS AND SONS

Now move into the chorus:

> It's a bridge you can't cross
> It's a cross you can't bear
> It's the words you can't say
> The things you can't change
> No matter how much you care
> So you do all you can
> Then you've got let go
> You're just part of the flow
> Of the river that runs between FATHERS AND SONS

We see the first chorus from the son's point of view, colored only by the son's eyes. Now the second system is free to look from the other side of the river:

> Now when I look at my own son

I know what my father went through
There's only so much you can do
You're proud when they walk
Scared when they run
That's how it always has been between FATHERS AND SONS

It's a bridge you can't cross
It's a cross you can't bear
It's the words you can't say
The things you can't change
No matter how much you care
So you do all you can
Then you've got let go
You're just part of the flow
Of the river that runs between FATHERS AND SONS

The father's perspective colors the second chorus. It becomes, for me at least, more interesting than the first chorus. Here is a simple principle for division of labor: Put separate ideas in separate systems.

The problem in *Fathers and Sons* is that both ideas are in the first system, leaving the lyric no place new to go. Separating the ideas into separate systems makes both systems fresh.

This principle for the division of labor has practical applications. Say you are writing a lyric whose summary is: Our lives without each other are sad. We should be together.

It contains three perspectives: 1. I (me), 2. you, 3. we. This clearly suggests a division of labor for the verses:

Verse 1: I have become a monk in the Himalayas: the only way I can find peace.
Verse 2: You are seeking fulfillment working with the Sisters of Mercy.
Verse 3: We need to talk this over . . .

This is the old I-you-we formula for lyric development: each verse focuses from a different point of view. It's a nice guideline for dividing your verses' jobs. Sometimes it'll be just what you need, other times, like any formula, it will take the freshness out of your writing. Be aware of it, just don't make it a habit.

SECOND VERSE HELL

Figuring out where to go after the first chorus is one of the hardest (and most persistent) problems that songwriters face. You face it every time you write a song, unless your song is only one system long. It's called second verse hell.

Look at this lyric by Pat Alger, Garth Brooks and Larry B. Bastain. The first two verses set up a clear situation:

UNANSWERED PRAYERS

Just the other night at a hometown football game
My wife and I ran into my old high school flame
And as I introduced them the past came back to me
And I couldn't help but think of the way things used to be

She was the one that I'd wanted for all times
And each night I'd spend prayin' that God would make her mine
And if he'd only grant me that wish I'd wished back then
I'd never ask for anything again

Now comes the punch line:

Sometimes I thank God for UNANSWERED PRAYERS
Remember when you're talkin' to the man upstairs
That just because he doesn't answer doesn't mean he don't care
Some of God's greatest gifts are UNANSWERED PRAYERS

With all the information we have so far, it's a little difficult to see how to develop the story much further. Here's verse three:

She wasn't quite the angel that I remembered in my dreams
And I could tell that time had changed me in her eyes too it seemed
We tried to talk about the old days, there wasn't much we could recall
I guess the Lord knows what he's doin' after all

Now follow it with the chorus:

Sometimes I thank God for UNANSWERED PRAYERS
Remember when you're talkin' to the man upstairs
That just because he doesn't answer doesn't mean he don't care
Some of God's greatest gifts are UNANSWERED PRAYERS

Is there anything gained? Not much. We already knew, from the combination of the first two verses and the chorus, how thankful he was not to be with his old girlfriend. This verse just elaborates on the same theme, giving us a few more details, including the old girlfriend's attitude. And the final line, "I guess the Lord knows what he's doin' after all," just repeats the idea, "just because he doesn't answer doesn't mean he don't care."

In short, the second chorus is destined to die an ignominious death right there in front of everybody. Now the song moves into a bridge, followed by a third chorus:

> And as she walked away I looked at my wife
> And then and there I thanked the Good Lord for the gifts in my life
>
> Sometimes I thank God for UNANSWERED PRAYERS
> Remember when you're talkin' to the man upstairs
> That just because he doesn't answer doesn't mean he don't care
> Some of God's greatest gifts are UNANSWERED PRAYERS

STOP Much better. I had forgotten about the wife. The third chorus is interesting again; it changes color completely. Go back and read the bridge followed by the whole chorus.

The wife becomes God's greatest gift. A lovely payoff.

Two out of three choruses work great, but the song sags at the second chorus. There isn't enough new information in verse three to make the chorus interesting. Other than leaving it alone as good enough (two out of three ain't bad . . .), what would you do?

One possibility might be to re-introduce the wife in verse three and skip the bridge entirely, like this:

> She wasn't quite the angel that I remembered in my dreams
> And I could tell that time had changed me in her eyes too it seemed
> As she turned and walked away I looked at my wife
> And recognized the gift I'd been given in my life
>
> Sometimes I thank God for UNANSWERED PRAYERS
> Remember when you're talkin' to the man upstairs
> That just because he doesn't answer doesn't mean he don't care

Some of God's greatest gifts are UNANSWERED PRAYERS

Now the song is a simple three verse, two chorus layout with both choruses doing their work. Read the entire lyric and watch how each chorus changes:

UNANSWERED PRAYERS

Just the other night at a hometown football game
My wife and I ran into my old high school flame
And as I introduced them the past came back to me
And I couldn't help but think of the way things used to be

She was the one that I'd wanted for all times
And each night I'd spend prayin' that God would make her mine
And if he'd only grant me that wish I'd wished back then
I'd never ask for anything again

Sometimes I thank God for UNANSWERED PRAYERS
Remember when you're talkin' to the man upstairs
That just because he doesn't answer doesn't mean he don't care
Some of God's greatest gifts are UNANSWERED PRAYERS

She wasn't quite the angel that I remembered in my dreams
And I could tell that time had changed me in her eyes too it seemed
As she turned and walked away I looked at my wife
And recognized the gift I'd been given in my life

Sometimes I thank God for UNANSWERED PRAYERS
Remember when you're talkin' to the man upstairs
That just because he doesn't answer doesn't mean he don't care
Some of God's greatest gifts are UNANSWERED PRAYERS

Very effective movement.

OK, I lied. The original version of the lyric that I gave you isn't the way the song was recorded. They did try to do it as verse/verse/chorus, verse/chorus, bridge/chorus, but it made the song, in Pat Alger's words, "feel too long." Another way of saying the song sagged; lost interest. And what did they cut out? Here's their solution, as recorded by Garth Brooks:

UNANSWERED PRAYERS

Just the other night at a hometown football game
My wife and I ran into my old high school flame
And as I introduced them the past came back to me
And I couldn't help but think of the way things used to be

She was the one that I'd wanted for all times
And each night I'd spend prayin' that God would make her mine
And if he'd only grant me that wish I'd wished back then
I'd never ask for anything again

Sometimes I thank God for UNANSWERED PRAYERS
Remember when you're talkin' to the man upstairs
That just because he doesn't answer doesn't mean he don't care
Some of God's greatest gifts are UNANSWERED PRAYERS

She wasn't quite the angel that I remembered in my dreams
And I could tell that time had changed me in her eyes too it seemed
We tried to talk about the old days, there wasn't much we could recall
I guess the Lord knows what he's doin' after all

And as she walked away I looked at my wife
And then and there I thanked the Good Lord for the gifts in my life

Sometimes I thank God for UNANSWERED PRAYERS
Remember when you're talkin' to the man upstairs
That just because he doesn't answer doesn't mean he don't care
Some of God's greatest gifts are UNANSWERED PRAYERS

They left out the second chorus and went immediately to the bridge—an unusual formal move, especially in commercial music. But it works: both choruses shine and we stay interested in the song all the way through.

Keeping the bridge gives the music a chance to breathe, since the verses lines are long and the tempo is slow. Creating a contrasting section helps the overall flow of the song. The formal risk pays off, creating interest and contrast at the same time. Put this move in your toolbox. It could come in handy.

Of course, there are no rules. The solution to the question "Where do I go now?" changes with every song. Sometimes it's even the wrong question. Just because you wrote a verse first doesn't mean it's the first verse. Instead of asking "Where do I go now?" it may help to ask "Where did I get here from?" Get used to juggling and trying new things.

EXERCISE

Here's your assignment: Write three verses, each one ending with the same line (call it a refrain) which includes the title. It's really a three system song: verse/refrain, verse/refrain, verse/refrain.

Each verse/refrain system should advance the storyline to the next place. One easy way is to create a story that moves chronologically through time, perhaps from past to present. Like this:

1. He volunteered to serve his country in the Great War.
2. In the trenches he suffered from shell shock and battle fatigue.
3. Back home he can't even hear a door slam without losing control.

You could work non-chronologically:

1. Back home he can't even hear a door slam without losing control.
2. He volunteered to serve his country in the Great War.
3. In the trenches he suffered from shell shock and battle fatigue.

or even

1. Back home he can't even hear a door slam without losing control.
2. In the trenches he suffered from shell shock and battle fatigue.
3. He volunteered to serve his country in the Great War.

In the non-chronological cases, "had" shows the earlier past. The distinction is also made by the acts themselves: First you volunteer, then you serve, then you feel the after-effects.

If I were writing this lyric, I'd do some research on World War I and life in the trenches. I'd look for image words that work not only for the trenches (verse two) but for the other sections as well.

Wherever these words appeared, they would connect ("cluster with") other parts of the lyric to create a continuity of tone and idea. Here are some possibilities:

Rockets exploding overhead
Layers of dust from rocket explosions covering everything in the morning
Hiding underground in caves during aerial bombardment
Gas masks, mustard gas, fog

You could do some Object Writing on each of these to get something from your own sense pool. You could also treat them as metaphors for something else. (Right now, I'm tempted to revise or eliminate the section about volunteering so I can go back to his childhood.)

Ideally, I'll end up with a list of words that evoke the trenches or their home-bound counterparts that I can use throughout the lyric. The more specific they are, the more effective they will be. Keep them sense-bound (seven-senses; remember?).

Now, find a refrain that can appear productively in the same place in each verse. If I were to look for a refrain for the Great War idea that could work for all three sections. I would be attracted to something like *Ashes, ashes, all fall down.*

It works for a childhood section, also for the ashen faces of the shell-shocked soldiers, the dust from the rockets and gunpowder. I'd have to find an angle for the third section, but it shouldn't be too difficult. He certainly could tumble like a child when the door slams.

Go ahead and write it. Remember that all your verses should have their own jobs to do. Use *Ashes, ashes, all fall down* as your refrain. Above all, take your time. This is a process. Enjoy it.

Chapter Six

Verse Development and Power Positions

♪♪♪

T hink of your verses as colored spotlights. They shine their lights on their chorus or refrain. If two verses project the same color, their choruses will look the same. If they project different colors, the choruses will look different. Keep your verses interesting and keep your idea moving forward. You'll have little trouble lighting up your chorus or refrain in different ways. You don't have to use formulas. You don't have to introduce a whole new cast of characters. You just have to pay attention.

Let's look at the verse development in Beth Nielsen Chapman's *Child Again*. Each verse projects a different color on its chorus, changing our way of seeing it, keeping it interesting. We'll look at two areas of this lovely lyric:

1. Its use of *repetition*. Because of strong verse development, the chorus changes to a new and more interesting color each time we see it.
2. Its *power positions* light up the chorus with the right color from the right angle to put crucial ideas in the strongest focus.

Here is the lyric, from her Reprise album *Beth Nielsen Chapman:*

CHILD AGAIN

Verse 1

She's wheeled into the hallway
Till the sun moves down the floor
Little squares of daylight

Like a hundred times before
She's taken to the garden
For the later afternoon
Just before her dinner
They return her to her room

Chorus 1

And inside her mind
She is running in the summer wind
Inside her mind
She is running in the summer wind
Like a CHILD AGAIN

Verse 2

The family comes on Sundays
And they hover for a while
They fill her room with chatter
And they form a line of smiles
Children of her children
Bringing babies of their own
Sometimes she remembers
Then her mama calls her home

Chorus 2

And inside her mind
She is running in the summer wind
Inside her mind
She is running in the summer wind
Like a CHILD AGAIN

Bridge (duet)

It's raining it's pouring	It's raining
The old man is snoring	Come out and play with me
Bumped his head on the edge of the bed	And bring your dollies three
And he couldn't get up in the morning.	Climb up my apple tree
Rain rain go away	Slide down my rain barrel
Come again another day	Into my cellar door

Little Johnny wants to play And we'll be jolly friends
Some more Forever more

Chorus 3
And inside her mind
She is running in the summer wind
Inside her mind
She is running in the summer wind
Like a CHILD AGAIN

First System Focus

The first verse contains three scenes, each one showing the old woman being taken somewhere. She is physically helpless, a focus firmly established right away:

Verse 1
She's wheeled into the hallway
Till the sun moves down the floor
Little squares of daylight
Like a hundred times before

This helplessness is reiterated by the following two scenes:

She's taken to the garden
For the later afternoon

Just before her dinner
They return her to her room

These three scenes color the first chorus with helplessness: we see her helpless in the nursing home, being taken everywhere, but

Chorus 1
Inside her mind
She is running in the summer wind
Inside her mind
She is running in the summer wind
Like a CHILD AGAIN

We enter the chorus knowing her situation, and are swept back to a time when she was "running in the summer wind/ Like a CHILD AGAIN."

Since the verse puts her in a wheelchair, being *taken* and *returned*, we can't help but see *running* as a contrast. We interpret the chorus in the light of the verse.

Second System Focus

The second system turns the color of her relatives.

Verse 2
> The family comes on Sundays
> And they hover for a while
> They fill her room with chatter
> And they form a line of smiles

What terrific lines. Four generations are present in her room; no doubt she has little connection with the younger generations, nor do they have much with her.

> Children of her children
> Bringing babies of their own

She tries to pay attention, but her mind wanders off . . .

> Sometimes she remembers
> Then her mama calls her home

Chorus 2
> And inside her mind
> She is running in the summer wind

When the chorus repeats, we see her as a child with her own mother, a color carefully arranged by the second verse's focus on family. The emphasis is no longer on her running, but on the family (her mama) that she runs to, surrounded as she is by strangers. The second chorus lights up brilliantly, a new and different color made possible by strong verse development.

The bridge (an overlay of old-fashioned childrens' songs) is the coup de grâce. It shows us the colors of childhood inside her mind, or, more accurately, inside our own minds when we were children.

Bridge

It's raining it's pouring	It's raining
The old man is snoring	Come out and play with me
Bumped his head on the edge of the bed	And bring your dollies three
And he couldn't get up in the morning.	Climb up my apple tree
Rain rain go away	Slide down my rain barrel
Come again another day	Into my cellar door
Little Johnny wants to play	And we'll be jolly friends
Some more	Forever more

And inside her mind
She is running in the summer wind
Inside her mind
She is running in the summer wind
Like a CHILD AGAIN

In our third and final look at the chorus, we see her with new eyes. We see where she really is, back again with mama, able to run home. Reality is doubled and reflected, colored by our knowledge that she is destined to follow her own mother all too soon, as inevitably as the generations crowding into her room will follow her. That is part of the point of showing us the children in the second verse, then showing her as a child running to mama.

Many families visit relatives in nursing homes, and most leave saddened. "She's losing it. She didn't even remember us . . . ". But to see their loved one in this new light for the first time "running in the summer wind/ Like a CHILD AGAIN" is an emotional revelation. It is this startling insight into the mind of the old woman that lights up radio station switchboards wherever *Child Again* is aired.

POWER POSITIONS

The opening and closing lines of any lyric section are naturally strong. They are bathed in spotlights. If you want people to notice an important idea, put it in the lights of a power position, and you will communicate the idea more forcefully. (For a full treatment of power positions, see my book, *Managing Lyric Structure*.) Look at the opening line of *Child Again: She's wheeled into the hallway*.

Closing lines are also power positions, another place to light up an important idea. In this case, the closing line prepares us to enter the chorus. I call it a trigger position, because it releases us into the chorus carrying whatever the line says with us, and therefore we see the chorus in the light of the idea, *They return her to her room*.

Look at the first line and the last line in combination, and you'll see how they focus the meaning of the chorus:

> She's wheeled into the hallway
> They return her to her room
>
> And inside her mind
> She is running in the summer wind . . .
> Like a CHILD AGAIN

Look at verse one carefully, and you'll see that it really contains two parts. The rhythm is basic common meter (like *Mary had a little lamb*), alternating first and third long phrases with shorter phrases in the second and fourth positions.

	rhyme	stresses
She's whéeled ínto the hállway	×	3+
While the sún moves dówn the flóor	a	3
Líttle squáres of dáylight	×	3+
Like a húndred tímes befóre	a	3

After these four lines, things are balanced. The structure has resolved. This creates a new beginning at line five—another power position. Look how it's used:

> She's taken to the garden
> For the later afternoon
> Just before her dinner
> They return her to her room

Taken is the first stressed syllable. Of the eight lines in the verse, two are opening positions, and two are closing positions. Look at the entire verse and see what messages the power positions communicate:

Verse 1

> She's wheeled into the hallway
> While the sun moves down the floor
> Little squares of daylight
> Like a hundred times before
> She's taken to the garden
> For the later afternoon
> Just before her dinner
> They return her to her room

Ms. Chapman has made sure we will enter the first chorus from the angle of physical helplessness. She uses her power positions—the first and last positions of the verse, plus the ending and beginning of its subsections—to lock our focus in, forcing us to see the first chorus the color she wants us to. Neat.

Not So Powerful Power Positions

Look what happens with different ideas in the power positions:

Verse 1

> While the sun moves down hallway
> She's wheeled out from her room
> So many times she's been there
> As the squares of daylight move
> Then later in the garden
> She's taken out of doors
> They return her for her dinner
> Down the hallway's polished floors

Chorus 1

> And inside her mind
> She is running in the summer wind . . .
> Like a CHILD AGAIN

Even though the beauty of the original verse has suffered, the ideas haven't really changed, only their placement has changed. Look at the information in the power positions now:

>   While the sun moves down hallway
>   As the squares of daylight move
>   Then later in the garden
>   Down the hallway's polished floors

Chorus 1
>   And inside her mind
>   She is running in the summer wind . . .

Because the power positions focus us elsewhere, the chorus seems to stress her escape from routine rather than her physical disability.

Power Positions in Verse Two

The second verse introduces a different color with it's opening and closing phrases:

>   The family comes on Sundays
>   Then her mama calls her home

This verse shifts focus to her room, where she is surrounded on Sundays by family visitors. They are *external* to her, shown by the brilliant metaphor closing the first subsection:

>   And they form a line of smiles

The family visits, mostly with each other. They are probably sad that she's "so out of touch," even though some of them are virtual strangers, four generations away.

>   Children of her children

The family seems almost oblivious as she seems to slip in and out of their reality. They don't have a clue of where she really is. The trigger line sets up the contrast between external and internal.

Verse 2
>   The family comes on Sundays
>   And they hover for a while

They fill her room with chatter
And they form a line of smiles
Children of her children
Bringing babies of their own
Sometimes she remembers
Then her mama calls her home

Chorus 2
And inside her mind
She is running in the summer wind . . .
Like a CHILD AGAIN

The power positions in this verse force the new color onto the chorus. Outside, the generations chatter on; inside lies a place of peace, memory and happiness.

Each verse works beautifully to set up its special view of the chorus. The accumulation of the two systems delivers the knock-out:

Verse 1
She's wheeled into the hallway
Like a hundred times before
She's taken to the garden
They return her to her room

Chorus 1
And inside her mind
She is running in the summer wind . . .
Like a CHILD AGAIN

Verse 2
The family comes on Sundays
And they form a line of smiles
Children of her children
Then her mama calls her home

Chorus 2
And inside her mind
She is running in the summer wind . . .
Like a CHILD AGAIN

Because her body is helpless, because she is frustrated by the world her relatives seem so comfortable in, she seeks comfort in a kinder, gentler place away from boredom, routine and frustration.

After the bridge shows us the colors of childhood again with her, old age becomes accessible: finally we understand. The power of a perfectly developed song: It changes our way of looking at our lives and our surroundings.

More Power Positions

Opening and closing phrases are not the only way to create power positions. Wherever you create a special effect with your structure, you call attention to what you are saying. This extra focus gives the position its power. This one creates several power positions:

> Mary had a little lamb
> Its fleece was white as snow
> And everywhere that Mary went
> The lamb would go, indeed
> He goes wherever Mary leads
> He follows with devoted speed

The opening phrase, as usual, is a power position. So is the fourth phrase, since it closes the section. But it gains extra punch by rhyming early, at the second rather than the third stress. Phrase five is unexpected, adding special interest. The final phrase is the most powerful of the bunch.

Look at all the power generated in this pretty structure by Jim Rushing:

When I left I left walking wounded	x
I made my escape from the rain	a
Still a prisoner of hurt	b
I had months worth of work	b
Freeing my mind of the pain	a
I had hours of sitting alone in the dark	c
Listening to sad songs and coming apart	c
Lord knows I made crying an art	c
Weak is a SLOW HEALING HEART	c

When the third phrase ends short, the acceleration gets our attention. Then the fourth phrase chimes in, and the fifth phrase closes with a rhyme. Six is another opening and calls extra attention to its length. I could argue that seven is a power position too, but I won't. Five out of nine is plenty of action, a tribute to interesting structures.

Moral: first be aware of where your power positions are: opening positions, closing positions, and surprises, like shorter, longer, or extra lines. Pay attention as you create them, then put something important there. Everything will come up rosy, seafoam green, tangiers blue, sun yellow . . .

Chapter Seven

Travelogues
Verse Continuity

We've all seen travelogues. Ah, fabulous Hawaii. Majestic mountains, pipeline surfing, luxury hotels. The places may be interesting, but as a film, a travelogue is dull, dull, dull. Its elements have no natural continuity. What do majestic mountains have to do with twenty-foot waves featuring pipeline surfing? What have either of these to do with elegant hotels and Oriental cuisine? Their only links are accidents of geography: they are all part of fabulous Hawaii!

A travelogue not only makes for a dull movie, it makes for dull verse development in a lyric. Look at this:

Verse 1: Police brutality is a common problem in large cities.
Refrain: Streets are turning deadly in the dark.

Verse 2: Car bombs are becoming more common as a terrorist weapon.
Refrain: Streets are turning deadly in the dark.

Verse 3: More prostitutes carry the AIDS virus every year.
Refrain: Streets are turning deadly in the dark.

What's going on here? What does police brutality have to do with car bombs or prostitutes with AIDS. Nothing, except that they are all part of fabulous *Streets are turning deadly in the dark.* Aside from their connection to the refrain, the elements have no natural relationship—don't belong together.

Verse development should mean verse relationship. Your verses should have a good reason to hang out together. When verses are in the same lyric only because you're taking a tour of the title, you likely have a travelogue on your hands.

OK, so no one would actually write something like that, right? Wrong. It happens all the time, all too often in songs with serious political, ethical, or religious messages. This series of ideas is typical:

Verse 1: We're screwing up our planet.
Refrain: We're losing the human race.

Verse 2: We're killing each other in stupid wars.
Refrain: We're losing the human race.

Verse 3: We ignore our poor and homeless.
Refrain: We're losing the human race.

No matter how well written and interesting these verses get, the basic defect remains: the verses don't work together to accumulate power—they are simply a travelogue of human ineptitude. Important ideas deserve the most powerful presentation you can muster.

Your lyric accumulates power when your verses work together—using each verse to prepare what comes next. It's like starting avalanches. If you go a third of the way up the mountain and start three separate avalanches from different spots, you'll cause some damage to the town below, but not nearly as much as if you'd gone to the top and rolled one snowball all the way down. Speed and power accumulate and sweep everything away. The town is devastated.

Time to get to work. We'll start by putting together a travelogue (on a serious subject) and then we'll try to fix it. Let's work with the idea of cycles of violence, using *Chain Reaction* as a title. Here's a starting verse and chorus:

CHAIN REACTION
Verse 1
    Louis ducks behind the door
    Patient as a stone

Listens, braces, hears the footsteps
Crip for sure and all alone
Steel barking, flashing, biting
Sinking to its home
Flesh to blood to heart to bone

One more link in a CHAIN REACTION
Spinning round and round and round
A tiny step, a small subtraction
One more link in a CHAIN REACTION

OK, gang warfare. One violent act will surely lead to another. But instead of using this scene to move us to the next act in the chain, we'll let the lyric make the easy move and randomly select another place. Violence is, after all, easy to find. Here we are in someplace like fabulous West Beirut:

Verse 2

Camille slips along the wall
Muslims stand their posts
Pulls the pin and lobs the metal
Perfect hook shot, crowd explodes
Spilling colors red and khaki
Gargles in their throats
Infidels and pagan hosts

One more link in a CHAIN REACTION
Spinning round and round and round
A tiny step, a small subtraction
One more link in a CHAIN REACTION

However compelling the scene is, it is isolated; a single snowball a third of the way up the mountain. Because it relates to verse one only through the chorus, it doesn't build momentum. Its only power comes from what it is, not what it connects to. Verse one was a separate avalanche. It lent no power to verse two.

Now, one last stop in this travelogue of violence. How about racial hatred in fabulous old South Africa?

Verse 3

White boys rock the ancient Ford

Teeter totter swing
Trapped inside, the children shudder
Afrikaner ditties ring
Drag a papa, slag a mama
Flames that lick and stink
Little buggers boil like ink

One more link in a CHAIN REACTION
Spinning round and round and round
A tiny step, a small subtraction
One more link in a CHAIN REACTION

It's not that a lyric like this has no power, it just doesn't have the power it could have. Even when each scene in a travelogue is effectively presented, there is less total impact than there could have been if each verse had carried over into the next, accumulating power and momentum

The test is to look at the verses without the chorus. Without knowing that all three events take place in fabulous CHAIN RE-ACTION, we wouldn't have a clue what's going on:

Verse 1

Louis ducks behind the door
Patient as a stone
Listens, braces, hears the footsteps
Crip for sure and all alone
Steel barking, flashing, biting
Sinking to its home
Flesh to blood to heart to bone

Verse 2

Camille slips along the wall
Muslims at their posts
Pulls the pin and lobs the metal
Perfect hook shot, crowd explodes
Spilling colors red and khaki
Gargles in their throats
Infidels and pagan hosts

Verse 3

    White boys rock the ancient Ford
    Teeter totter swing
    Trapped inside the children shudder
    Afrikaner ditties ring
    Drag the papa, slag the mama
    Flames that lick and stink
    Little buggers boil like ink

Now, instead, we'll try developing one continuous fabric. It doesn't matter which verse we pick, just so all the other verses roll down the same mountain with it. Let's start with verse one and develop from there.

CHAIN REACTION

Verse 1

    Louis ducks behind the door
    Patient as a stone
    Listens, braces, hears the footsteps
    Crip for sure and all alone
    Steel barking, flashing, biting
    Sinking to its home
    Flesh to blood to heart to bone

    One more link in a CHAIN REACTION
    Spinning round and round and round
    A tiny step, a small subtraction
    One more link in a CHAIN REACTION

Verse 2

    Straightens up now cool and thin
    Checking out his score
    That's for Iggy, dirty bastard
    Gargled blood in memory's roar
    Circle turf in hasty exit
    One more hero born
    Mamas screaming dark and torn

    One more link in a CHAIN REACTION
    Spinning round and round and round

Another turn, another fraction
One more link in a CHAIN REACTION

Verse 3
Gathered hands in rings of steel
They weld a sacred vow
Swing down low, chariot wheeling
Rolling dark across the town
Mad archangel's scabbard flashing
Cut another down
Driving by on bloody ground

One more link in a CHAIN REACTION
Spinning round and round and round
Another turn, another fraction
One more link in a CHAIN REACTION

The linking of the verses gives the whole lyric momentum.
Look at the results when we leave out the chorus:

Verse 1
Louis ducks behind the door
Patient as a stone
Listens, braces, hears the footsteps
Crip for sure and all alone
Steel barking, flashing, biting
Sinking to its home
Flesh to blood to heart to bone

Verse 2
Straightens up now cool and thin
Checking out his score
That's for Iggy, dirty bastard
Gargled blood in memory's roar
Circle turf in hasty exit
One more hero born
Mamas screaming dark and torn

Verse 3
Gathered hands in rings of steel

They weld a sacred vow
Swing down low, chariot wheeling
Rolling dark across the town
Mad archangel's scabbard flashing
Cut another down
Driving by on bloody ground

Now the verses show the circle of violence, and the chorus gains power each time because the information carries over from verse to verse, adding weight and momentum to each scene.

EXERCISE

Your turn. Start with either verse two or verse three of the original and write two more verses to make a story. (Keep the same chorus, and be sure to follow the current verse rhyme scheme and rhythm.) You'll notice the power and momentum your lyric develops as the verses accumulate into one full-blown strategy.

Verse development is probably the lyricist's trickiest job. Verse ideas must advance enough, but can't move too much. If the ideas are too close, the repetition of the chorus will become static and boring. If the verses' ideas are too far apart, you might end up in fabulous Hawaii. Hawaii is a nice place, but songwriters, beware how you get there. The best trip is paid for by royalty checks from great songs.

Chapter Eight

Stripping Your Repetition for Repainting

♪♩♪♪

Strong verse development is crucial to recoloring your repetition. Just as important, however, is making sure your repetitive section (your refrain or your chorus) can be recolored. Sometimes it can resist recoloring, no matter how well your verses develop.

Here you are, cruising along in your lyric, delighted by its possibilities:

> Exploding from the starting blocks
> Again he set the pace
> Though he was crowned by laurel wreaths
> As thousands cheered he came to grief
> He lost the human race

Yessirree, what a refrain! Even a double meaning! Of course, now you have to face second verse hell: trying to figure out what to say next so the refrain will be as interesting the second time as it was the first. Hmmm.

> It's hard see through miles ahead
> To shoulders bent by age
> With crowds of whispers drawing tight
> He'll tilt his head one final night

Oops! You can't say *He lost the human race.* It won't go with *He'll tilt his head one final night.* The refrain has to change:

> It's hard see through miles ahead
> To shoulders bent by age
> With crowds of whispers drawing tight
> He'll tilt his head one final night
> He'll lose the human race

Though this isn't the kiss of death, avoid changing the refrain if you can.

A good lyric works hard for interesting verse development that colors the refrain a new shade each time, so it's frustrating when a refrain proves to be color resistant, protected from the verses by coats and coats of verbal polyurethane. Too often, a problem with verb tense or an inconsistent point of view (POV) blocks effective coloring.

You can often solve the problem by neutralizing the refrain's tense and POV—stripping away protective coatings so your refrain can accept the colors the verses try to paint it.

NEUTRALIZING TENSES

Verbs determine tenses:

Past: He lost the human race

Present: He loses the human race

Future: He'll lose the human race

Controlling verbs is the key to controlling tense. Here are three ways:

1. Use the *ing* form of the verb (e.g., *losing*). Omit any helping verbs (*losing* instead of *is losing, was losing, will be losing*). Don't mistake the *ing* verb form for verbal adjectives (participles), e.g., *a losing strategy*, or for verbal nouns (gerunds), e.g., *Losing builds character*.
2. Use the *to* form of the verb (infinitive) and omit the main verb, e.g., *to lose* rather than *I hate to lose*.
3. Omit verbs altogether.

A tense *neutral* refrain will accept whatever tense the verse throws at it. Look at what the *ing* verb form does for our refrain, no matter what tense the verse takes:

Past tense:

> Exploding from the starting blocks
> Again he set the pace
> Though he was crowned by laurel wreaths
> As thousands cheered he came to grief
> Losing the human race

Present tense:

> Exploding from the starting blocks
> Again he sets the pace
> Although he's crowned by laurel wreaths
> As thousands cheer he comes to grief
> Losing the human race

Future tense:

> Exploding from the starting blocks
> Again he'll set the pace
> Though he'll be crowned by laurel wreaths
> As thousands cheer he'll come to grief
> Losing the human race

Now let's add our second verse:

Present

> Exploding from the starting blocks
> Again he sets the pace
> Although he's crowned by laurel wreaths
> As thousands cheer he comes to grief
> Losing the human race

Future

> It's hard see through miles ahead
> To shoulders bent by age
> With crowds of whispers drawing tight
> He'll tilt his head one final night
> Losing the human race

The neutralized refrain works with the tense of both verses.
Let's try the infinitive:

Present

    Exploding from the starting blocks
    Again he sets the pace
    Although he's crowned by laurel wreaths
    As thousands cheer he comes to grief
    To lose the human race

Future

    It's hard see through miles ahead
    To shoulders bent by age
    With crowds of whispers drawing tight
    He'll tilt his head one final night
    To lose the human race

Again, the neutralized refrain accepts any tense. Whichever results you like better, the *ing* form or the infinitive, it's nice to have the option. Let's try the third technique—leaving out the verb altogether. In this case, it makes the refrain sound like a commentary:

Present

    Exploding from the starting blocks
    Again he sets the pace
    Although he's crowned by laurel wreaths
    As thousands cheer he comes to grief
    A loss of the human race

Future

    It's hard see through miles ahead
    To shoulders bent by age
    With crowds of whispers drawing tight
    He'll tilt his head one final night
    A loss of the human race

Not quite as strong in this case. Try all three options. Use whichever feels best.

NEUTRALIZING POINT OF VIEW

Pronouns determine point of view:

    1st Person: I lose the human race

2nd Person: You lose the human race

3rd Person: She loses the human race

To strip your refrain's POV, omit pronouns. Sometimes you'll have to neutralize verb tenses too. We'll look at this later.

Look back at our tense-neutral refrain, "Losing the human race." It not only neutralizes the verb, it also omits pronouns, freeing each verse to set its own POV. The neutral refrain accepts them all. Watch.

1st Person: (singular)
> Exploding from the starting blocks
> Again I set the pace
> Although I'm crowned by laurel wreaths
> As thousands cheer I'll come to grief
> Losing the human race

1st Person: (plural)
> Exploding from the starting blocks
> Again we set the pace
> Although we're crowned by laurel wreaths
> As thousands cheer we'll come to grief
> Losing the human race

2nd Person:
> Exploding from the starting blocks
> Again you set the pace
> Although you're crowned by laurel wreaths
> As thousands cheer you'll come to grief
> Losing the human race

3rd Person: (singular)
> Exploding from the starting blocks
> Again she sets the pace
> Although she's crowned by laurel wreaths
> As thousands cheer she'll come to grief
> Losing the human race

3rd Person: (plural)
    Exploding from the starting blocks
    Again they set the pace
    Although they're crowned by laurel wreaths
    As thousands cheer they'll come to grief
    Losing the human race

When you use third person with present tense, the verb adds an *s*: She loses. If you don't use *he, she, it* in your lyric, none of your verbs will add an *s*, so your verbs will all already be POV neutral. You won't need to neutralize the verbs—you just need to drop the pronouns:

1st Person: (singular)
    Exploding from the starting blocks
    Again I set the pace
    Although I'm crowned by laurel wreaths
    As thousands cheer I'll come to grief
    And lose the human race

1st Person: (plural)
    Exploding from the starting blocks
    Again we set the pace
    Although we're crowned by laurel wreaths
    As thousands cheer we'll come to grief
    And lose the human race

2nd Person:
    Exploding from the starting blocks
    Again you set the pace
    Although you're crowned by laurel wreaths
    As thousands cheer you'll come to grief
    And lose the human race

3rd Person: (plural)
    Exploding from the starting blocks
    Again they set the pace
    Although they're crowned by laurel wreaths
    As thousands cheer they'll come to grief
    And lose the human race

Be careful though. *And lose the human race* works only in *present tense*. If you change to past, you're in trouble:

3rd Person: (plural)
>   Exploding from the starting blocks
>   Again they set the pace
>   Though they were crowned by laurel wreaths
>   As thousands cheered they came to grief
>   And lose the human race

You'd need to neutralize the verb tense too, back to losing the human race.

Now, the real thing. Paul Simon's refrain "Still crazy after all these years" has no pronouns and no verb. The result is a refrain that can accept the POV and tense from each verse:

STILL CRAZY AFTER ALL THESE YEARS
>   I met my old lover on the street last night
>   She seemed so glad to see me, I just smiled
>   And we talked about some old times
>   And we drank ourselves some beers
>   Still crazy after all these years
>
>   I'm not the kind of man who tends to socialize
>   I seem to lean on old familiar ways
>   But I ain't no fool for love songs
>   That whisper in my ears
>   Still crazy after all these years
>
>   Now I sit by the window and I watch the cars
>   I fear I'll do some damage one fine day
>   But I would not be convicted
>   By a jury of my peers
>   Still crazy after all these years

Because the refrain is stripped for action, the first verse is able to color it with three different POV's:

>   *I am* still crazy after all these years
>   *We were* still crazy after all these years

She was still crazy after all these years

All three work fine. The result is a productive ambiguity that adds to the spell of the lyric.

Verse two's possible interpretations: *I am* still crazy after all these years, or *you are* still crazy after all these years.

We can almost hear the jukebox whispering "Hey fella, you're still crazy about her after all these years." Again, the POV swabs multiple colors on the refrain, creating depth. In the third verse, my peers wouldn't convict me because *I would be* still crazy after all these years, or *They would be* still crazy after all these years.

I could cop a plea of insanity. *They* would understand, being, as my peers, crazy themselves. Again, the neutral refrain contributes productively to the ambiguity.

STRIPPING YOUR CHORUS

Neutralize a chorus the same way you neutralize a refrain: make sure you don't use a tense or point of view. Here's the prototype neutral chorus:

> Losing the human race
> Losing the human race
> Yeah, yeah, yeah
> Losing the human race

See how easily it works:

> Exploding from the starting blocks
> Again he sets the pace
> Although he's crowned by laurel wreaths
> As thousands cheer he comes to grief
> No reprieve

> *Chorus*
> Losing the human race
> Losing the human race
> Yeah, yeah, yeah
> Losing the human race

Like a refrain, a neutral chorus will accept the verse's tense and POV, no matter how many times you change them in the lyric. Remember as a rule of thumb, *verses show, chorus tells*. Keep your verses specific and interesting, and they will color abstract language with vivid swatches.

OK, the prototype chorus is pretty dumb. But you could easily add more interesting lines and find interesting rhymes. Make it as specific, imagistic and artistic as you want to, just don't commit to a tense or a POV. Like this:

Chorus
> Losing the human race
> Falling from heaven's grace
> No way to stop it
> Only a dot in space
> Losing the human race

None of the lines commit to tense or POV. They either use *ing* (lines one, two, and five), the infinitive (line three), or omit the verb altogether (line four). This stripped chorus will accept any POV and tense. Check out this one:

> Exploding from the starting blocks
> Again he sets the pace
> Although he's crowned by laurel wreaths
> As thousands cheer he comes to grief
> No reprieve

Chorus
> Losing the human race
> Falling from heaven's grace
> No way to stop it
> Only a dot in space
> Losing the human race

> He doesn't see the miles ahead
> Shoulders bent by age
> With crowds of whispers drawing tight
> He'll tilt his head one final night
> Slip from sight

Chorus

    Losing the human race
    Falling from heaven's grace
    No way to stop it
    Only a dot in space
    Losing the human race

Try it with a second person, past tense verse:

    Exploding from the starting blocks
    Again you set the pace
    Though you were crowned by laurel wreaths
    As thousands cheered you came to grief
    There was no reprieve

Chorus

    Losing the human race
    Falling from heaven's grace
    No way to stop it
    Only a dot in space
    Losing the human race

Again, the same chorus works fine. You don't have to neutralize your refrain or chorus for every lyric you write, but when your verses change tense and POV, it's good to know how to get your repetitive section ready for the new colors. This simple move, stripping away tense and POV, is often the key to success.

EXERCISE

As an exercise, neutralize the refrain *I fell too hard*. Don't read ahead until you're finished.

You should have three versions something like these: *falling too hard, to fall too hard,* and *too hard a fall.* Let your verses establish the tense and POV, and any of the three would work just fine. To finish off, I'll leave you with a chorus to neutralize. Have fun.

> I search for the good stuff
> I hope I can find enough
> I'm ready for love

Chapter Nine

Perspectives

♪♪♪

Whenever you put pen to paper you must choose how you will approach the world you are creating. You control your approach (and therefore your audience's) by choosing between the three main points of view: third person narrative, first person narrative, and second person or direct address. Each POV creates a world different from the others. Each has its own strengths and limitations. It is up to you to decide what will best serve your idea.

You write for an instrument—a singer who faces the audience and delivers your words. The point of view you choose controls the relationship between the singer and the audience. It sets the context for your ideas. Let's look at each point of view in turn.

In third person narrative the singer acts as a storyteller who simply directs the audience's attention to an objective world neither the singer nor the audience is a part of. They look together at a third thing, an objective, independent world.

You can tell third person by its pronouns:

	THIRD PERSON	
	Singular	**Plural**
Subject:	he, she, it	they
Direct Object:	him, her, it	them
Poss. Adjective:	his, her, its	their
Poss. Predicate:	his, hers, its	theirs

e.g. Possessive Adjective: "That is *her* responsibility."
Possessive Predicate: "The responsibility is *hers.*"

In third person narrative, both the singer and the audience

turn together to look at some third thing. The singer functions
only as storyteller or narrator.

THE GREAT PRETENDER
Yes, she's THE GREAT PRETENDER
Pretending that she's doing well
Her need is such, she pretends too much
She's lonely but no one can tell

Yes, she's THE GREAT PRETENDER
Adrift in a world of her own
She plays the game, but to her real shame
He's left her to dream all alone

Too real is her feeling of make-believe
Too real when she feels what her heart can't conceal

Yes, she's THE GREAT PRETENDER
Just laughing and gay like a clown
She seems to be what she's not, you see
She's wearing her heart like a crown
Pretending that he's still around

Imagine watching a singer perform the song. Either gender
could sing it, no problem. As an audience, we would look at the
pretender *with* the singer. Neither we nor the singer participates
in the world. Here's another example:

SENTIMENTAL LADY
The sidewalk runs from late day rainfall
Washes scraps of paper up against the grate
Backing up in shallow puddles
Oil floats like dirty rainbows
She hardly seems to notice as she steps across the street

Knows where she's headed for
She goes inside
Shuts the door

Chorus
SENTIMENTAL LADY
Doesn't mind it when it's raining
Doesn't seem to matter when it ends
SENTIMENTAL LADY
Sips her tea in perfect safety
Smiles her secret smile and pretends

Polished floors of blonde and amber
Hanging ivies lace her windows smooth and green
Soft inside these graceful patterns
Lost in thought she reads his letters
All that matters kept inside in memories and dreams

Knows where she has to be
Tucked away
Alone and free

Chorus
SENTIMENTAL LADY
Doesn't mind it when it's raining
Doesn't seem to matter when it ends
SENTIMENTAL LADY
Sips her tea in perfect safety
Smiles her secret smile and pretends

She made her mind up long ago
Not to look again
Her life was full
She sits content
Knows she's had its best

Chorus
SENTIMENTAL LADY
Doesn't mind it when it's raining
Doesn't seem to matter when it ends
SENTIMENTAL LADY
Sips her tea in perfect safety
Smiles her secret smile and pretends

FIRST PERSON

A first person narrative is also a storytelling mode, but instead of being separate from the action, the singer participates.

Here are the first person pronouns.

	FIRST PERSON	
	Singular	**Plural**
Subject:	I	we
Direct Object:	me	us
Poss. Adjective:	my	our
Poss. Predicate:	mine	ours

In a first person narrative, first person pronouns mix with third person pronouns.

THE GREAT PRETENDER

O yes *I'm* THE GREAT PRETENDER
Pretending that *I'm* doing well
My need is such, I pretend too much
I'm lonely but no one can tell

Yes *I'm* THE GREAT PRETENDER
Adrift in a world of *my* own
I play the game, but to *my* real shame
He's (or she's) left *me* to dream all alone

Too real is this feeling of make-believe
Too real when *I* feel what *my* heart can't conceal

Yes *I'm* THE GREAT PRETENDER
Just laughing and gay like a clown
I seem to be what *I'm* not, you see
I'm wearing *my* heart like a crown
Pretending that *he's (or she's)* still around

The singer is a participant, revealing something about him/ herself, so the gender of the singer and the pronouns will now make a difference.

DIGGING FOR THE LINE

My daddy loved the greyhounds

Oh he lived to watch 'em run
Breathless as they slow danced past
Like bullets from a gun
Muscles wound like springs of steel
Aching to unwind
Caught up in their rhythm
Daddy swayed in perfect time
Even when the chains of age
Left him weak and blind
He still could feel their rhythm
DIGGING FOR THE LINE

Even as a child I knew
The greyhounds never won
Though one of them might finish first
It wasn't why they'd run
Sliding on a rail of steel
A rabbit made of clay
Stayed up just ahead of them
Led the dancers all the way
Circle after circle
Panting just behind
They ran with grace and beauty
DIGGING FOR THE LINE

It hurt to see them run
A race they'd never win
But daddy smiled and made me see
This is what he said to me

A greyhound lives for running
It's the strongest drive he has
And though he never wins the race
The losing's not so bad
If he never ran at all
In time he'd surely die
The only world he cares to know
Is one that's always streaking by
It isn't what runs up ahead
It isn't what's behind

The beauty's in the way it feels
DIGGING FOR THE LINE

The narrator tells the story, but includes him/herself in it. In the last verse daddy speaks to the narrator while we are allowed to eavesdrop.

First Person Narrative

As an exercise, let's try changing *Sentimental Lady* into first person narrative.

SENTIMENTAL LADY

The sidewalk runs from late day rainfall
Washes scraps of paper up against the grate
Backing up in shallow puddles
Oil floats like dirty rainbows
I hardly seem to notice as I step across the street

Know where I'm headed for
I go inside
I shut the door

Chorus
SENTIMENTAL LADY
I don't mind it when it's raining
Doesn't seem to matter when it ends
SENTIMENTAL LADY
I sip my tea in perfect safety
Smile my secret smile and pretend

This sounds odd. She's saying external or descriptive things about herself, like, "I hardly seem to notice as I step across the street." Observations like this are best left to a third person narrator.

Polished floors of blonde and amber
Hanging ivies lace my windows smooth and green
Soft inside these graceful patterns
Lost in thought I read his letters
All that matters kept inside in memories and dreams

Know where I have to be
Tucked away
Alone and free

Chorus
SENTIMENTAL LADY
I don't mind it when it's raining
Doesn't seem to matter when it ends
SENTIMENTAL LADY
I sip my tea in perfect safety
Smile my secret smile and pretend

Again it sounds unnatural for her to say, "Lost in thought I read his letters." The language is more appropriate from the mouth of an observer than from the mouth of a participant. Finally, the bridge:

I made my mind up long ago
Not to look again
My life was full
I'll sit content
Knowing I've had its best

Chorus
SENTIMENTAL LADY
I don't mind it when it's raining
Doesn't seem to matter when it ends
SENTIMENTAL LADY
I sip my tea in perfect safety
Smile my secret smile and pretend

The bridge sounds natural in first person, since she's telling us something about herself we couldn't know from simply looking. Of course, looking into a character's mind is also perfectly appropriate in third person narrative.

If we really were to make sense of *Sentimental Lady* as a first person narrative, the perspective would have to shift in several places.

SENTIMENTAL LADY

The sidewalk runs from late day rainfall
Washes scraps of paper up against the grate
Backing up in shallow puddles
Oil floats like dirty rainbows
Splashed by cooling raindrops as I step across the street

I know what I'm headed for
Slip inside
Shut the door

Chorus

   I'm a SENTIMENTAL LADY
   I don't mind it when it's raining
   Doesn't *really* matter when it ends
   A SENTIMENTAL LADY
   Sipping tea in perfect safety
   Tucked away in secret with a friend

   I love these floors of blonde and amber
   Hanging ivies lace my windows smooth and green
   I live inside these graceful patterns
   Afternoons I read his letters
   All that matters here inside my memories and dreams

   Know where I *need* to be
   Tucked away
   Alone and free

Chorus

   I'm a SENTIMENTAL LADY
   I don't mind it when it's raining
   Doesn't really matter when it ends
   A SENTIMENTAL LADY
   Sipping tea in perfect safety
   Tucked away in secret with a friend

   I made my mind up long ago
   Not to look again
   My life was full

I sit content
Knowing I've had its best

Chorus
I'm a SENTIMENTAL LADY
I don't mind it when it's raining
Doesn't really matter when it ends
A SENTIMENTAL LADY
Sipping tea in perfect safety
Tucked away in secret with a friend

OK, so the rewrite could be more elegant. The point is that it works better. The trick is to put yourself in her mind—look from her perspective, and say what comes naturally.

Third Person Narrative

As a further exercise, go back and try changing *Digging for the Line* into a third person narrative. It's an interesting problem, isn't it? First there's the pronoun problem: you have to make daddy's child *she* to keep the *he's* from getting all jumbled together. Instead of:

His daddy loved the greyhounds
Oh he(?) lived to watch 'em run

you have to say

Her daddy loved the greyhounds
Oh he lived to watch 'em run

Even with that problem solved, you end up with a story about a father telling a story to his daughter. Seems a little complicated.

DIGGING FOR THE LINE
Her daddy loved the greyhounds
Oh he lived to watch 'em run
Breathless as they slow danced past
Like bullets from a gun
Muscles wound like springs of steel
Aching to unwind

Caught up in their rhythm
He swayed in perfect time
Even when the chains of age
Left him weak and blind
He still could feel their rhythm
DIGGING FOR THE LINE

Even as a child *she* knew
The greyhounds never won
Though one of them might finish first
It wasn't why they ran
Sliding on a rail of steel
A rabbit made of clay
Stayed up just ahead of them
Led the dancers all the way
Circle after circle
Panting just behind
They ran with grace and beauty
DIGGING FOR THE LINE

It hurt to see them run
A race they'd never win
But her daddy smiled and made her see
What it really means

He said, a greyhound lives for running
It's the strongest drive he has
And though he never wins the race
The losing's not so bad
If he never ran at all
In time he'd surely die
The only world he cares to know
Is one that's always streaking by
It isn't what runs up ahead
It isn't what's behind
The beauty's in the way it feels
DIGGING FOR THE LINE

Daddy told me this story is an acceptable premise for a song, but *here's a story about someone telling a story* seems more remote. The playwright Henrik Ibsen said, "If you put a gun in Act I, it damn well better go off by the end of the play!" This is more than a principle about effective use of props. It says that you should have a reason for each element in your work. Nothing without its purpose. No duplication of function.

Maybe the daughter is a gun that isn't going off. Let's see what happens if we eliminate her altogether:

DIGGING FOR THE LINE
Edwin loved the greyhounds
He lived to watch 'em run
Breathless as they slow danced past
Like bullets from a gun
Muscles wound like springs of steel
Aching to unwind
Caught up in their rhythm
He swayed in perfect time
Even when the chains of age
Left him weak and blind
He still could feel their rhythm
DIGGING FOR THE LINE

Even as a child *he* knew
The greyhounds never won
Though one of them might finish first
It wasn't why they ran
Sliding on a rail of steel
A rabbit made of clay
Stayed up just ahead of them
Led the dancers all the way
Circle after circle
Panting just behind
They ran with grace and beauty
DIGGING FOR THE LINE

It hurt to see them run
A race they'd never win
But as he grew old he learned to see
What it really means

A greyhound lives for running
It's the strongest drive he has
And though he never wins the race
The losing's not so bad
If he never ran at all
In time he'd surely die
The only world he cares to know
Is one that's always streaking by
It isn't what runs up ahead
It isn't what's behind
The beauty's in the way it feels
DIGGING FOR THE LINE

Much cleaner than with two characters. Simplify, simplify. Simplify. The only question now: which do you prefer, the first person narrative or the third person narrative? The key will be in the third verse. We will choose between listening in a more intimate situation to the singer telling us what he/she learned from daddy, or observing Edwin from a distance as he discovers the meaning of running:

FIRST PERSON NARRATIVE:	**THIRD PERSON NARRATIVE:**
But daddy smiled and made me see	But as he grew old he learned to see
This is what he said to me	What it really means
Son, a greyhound lives for running	A greyhound lives for running
It's the strongest drive he has	It's the strongest drive he has
And though he never wins the race	And though he never wins the race
The losing's not so bad	The losing's not so bad
If he never ran at all	If he never ran at all
In time he'd surely die	In time he'd surely die
The only world he cares to know	The only world he cares to know
Is one that's always streaking by	Is one that's always streaking by
It isn't what runs up ahead	It isn't what runs up ahead

It isn't what's behind	It isn't what's behind
The beauty's in the way it feels	The beauty's in the way it feels
DIGGING FOR THE LINE	DIGGING FOR THE LINE

In first person the singer as character/storyteller is right in front of us. We feel like we know him/her. But third person is cleaner and more focused in this case, because it eliminates a character. Your call.

SECOND PERSON

Second person is often called direct address because the singer (the first person, I) is talking to some second person (you), or maybe even right to the audience. Here are the pronouns.

	SECOND PERSON	
	Singular	**Plural**
Subject:	you	you
Direct Object:	you	you
Poss. Adjective:	your	your
Poss. Predicate:	yours	yours

Second person pronouns are mixed with first person pronouns to produce direct address—contact between *I* and *you*.

THE GREAT PRETENDER

Yes I'm THE GREAT PRETENDER
Adrift in a world of my own
I play the game, but to my real shame
You've left *me* to dream all alone

Too real is this feeling of make-believe
Too real when I feel what my heart can't conceal

Yes I'm THE GREAT PRETENDER
Just laughing and gay like a clown
I seem to be what I'm not, you see
I'm wearing my heart like a crown
Pretending that *you're* still around

The singer sings directly to a second person or persons (note that in English there is no difference between singular and plural, unless we resort to *y'all* or *youse* as plural forms—both forms intended as sophistications in a barren language that forgot to make the distinction). Because of the direct contact, second person is the most intimate of the points of view. As a listener,

I imagine the singer is singing to me, or
I watch the singer singing directly to someone else, real or imagined by the singer, or
I can imagine that the singer is someone I know singing to me, or
I can identify with the singer and sing to someone I know.

However I do it, it's pretty intimate. Below, the singer speaks to the image of someone in his past:

AS EACH YEAR ENDS

Becky Rose, you stole the night
Body dark, a sash of light
Soft you slippered from my bed
Not to wake me, dressing slow
How I watched I still don't know
I should have knelt and bowed to you instead

Chorus

AS EACH YEAR ENDS and one more breaks
I'll raise my wineglass high
To praise your beauty, you who touched my life
Though seasons bend, and colors fade
The memories still remain
I'll taste them once again AS EACH YEAR ENDS

Becky, how you broke my faith
Tearful as you pulled away
Dust of years and miles apart
Storms of summer rolled in slow
So hard it was, our letting go
That even now its shadows cross my heart

Chorus

AS EACH YEAR ENDS and one more breaks
I'll raise my wineglass high

To praise your beauty, you who touched my life
Though seasons bend, and colors fade
The memories still remain
I'll taste them once again AS EACH YEAR ENDS

Years like water join and run
Faces fade, too soon become
A taste of sadness on the tongue

Chorus
AS EACH YEAR ENDS and one more breaks
I'll raise my wineglass high
To praise your beauty, you who touched my life
Though seasons bend, and colors fade
The memories still remain
I'll taste them once again AS EACH YEAR ENDS

Even though Becky Rose is not in the singer's presence, it's still pretty intimate stuff. Compare it to a system of first person narrative:

Becky Rose stole the night
Her body dark, a sash of light
Soft *she* slippered from my bed
Not to wake me, dressing slow
How I watched I still don't know
I should have knelt and bowed to *her* instead

Chorus
AS EACH YEAR ENDS and one more breaks
I'll raise my wineglass high
To praise *her* beauty, *she* who touched my life
Though seasons bend, and colors fade
The memories still remain
I'll taste them once again AS EACH YEAR ENDS

Now look at the system as a third person narrative.

Becky Rose stole the night
Her body dark, a sash of light

Soft she slippered from *his* bed
Not to wake *him*, dressing slow
How *he* watched *he doesn't* know
He should have knelt and bowed to her instead

AS EACH YEAR ENDS and one more breaks
He raises his wineglass high
To praise her beauty, she who touched *his* life
Though seasons bend, and colors fade
The memories still remain
He tastes them once again AS EACH YEAR ENDS

What do you lose? Are there any gains? One thing changes: The chorus can be in present rather than future tense. A third person narrative can have a larger overview of time, stating simply, *"He tastes them once again* AS EACH YEAR ENDS."

From the first person, the singer promises to continue raising his glass: *"I'll taste them once again* AS EACH YEAR ENDS."

I don't have a problem making a choice here. I prefer the intimacy of Direct Address. Does that mean we should always go for intimacy?

 Try rewriting *Sentimental Lady* and *Digging for the Line* in direct address before you answer. Go on, do it.

As you can see, second person gets pretty complicated. The next two chapters will deal with some of its challenges.

Chapter Ten

Point of View:
Second Person and the Hangman

♪♪♪

J ust wait till your father gets home, young man!" said Mom, rolling her eyes in exasperation.

I was really going to get it. She'd tell Dad and I'd be lucky to see anything but my bedroom walls for weeks. More likely, this time I'd probably swing, twisting slowly in the wind.

Hours crawled by. Finally, the whirr of his Pontiac sliding into the driveway. Please God, let him suddenly remember something back at the office. Slam. Clomp clomp clomp.

Murmurs downstairs, then: "Come down for dinner, children." False sweetness in my executioner's voice. They're always nice right before they stretch your neck and watch your eyeballs pop. My sisters and I slid into our chairs, me reluctantly, them bright with expectation.

A casserole had never looked so gray, maybe tinged a little green. She let the minutes stack as Dad doused his cottage cheese with Tabasco sauce. I could hear the rope being flung over a high branch, checked for strength, the noose tested. Finally she spoke: "Well, young man, you've had quite a day today, haven't you?"

Aarrgh. That tightening sensation, breath coming harder.

"You're eleven years old, and should know better, shouldn't you?"

They always start by telling you how old you are.

"First, you sneak the BB gun out of the closet, where it is supposed to stay unless you have supervision!"

Dad chewed his cottage cheese and scowled; a dot of Tabasco sauce on his chin.

Why doesn't she just tell *him*? Why does she always have to say it to me?

"You could have stayed inside," she continued. "But oh no, mister smarty-pants, mister grown-up. You have to take it outside and shoot it! Were you aiming at Mister Nelson's window, trying to break it?"

Actually, I was trying to kill a bird. Never even noticed the window.

"You hit his living room mirror too, didn't you?"

Dad sat bolt upright, as though he felt someone going after his wallet.

She knew the facts and I knew the facts. The girls knew the facts. Dad was the only one who didn't know, so why was she telling me instead of him? More pleasure in the execution?

"And what did he say it would cost? *One hundred and seventy-two dollars*, that's what!" She sat back, sagging and weak from the burden of having me for a son. My sisters flushed with delight, pulling for the hangman.

Dad reddening and rising. The feeling of my feet leaving the floor, a tightening in my throat, and the sound of the wind in the trees . . .

Sometimes, lyrics sound like Mom. They seem to be talking directly to you, but are really telling someone else what you already know. Like this:

> I met you on a Saturday
> Your hair was wound in braids
> You walked up and you said hello
> And then you asked my name

This sounds unnatural because *you* already knows all this stuff. The verse is trying to do two things at once: tell the audience the facts, while pretending to carry on a conversation with *you*. Technically, we have a point of view problem: Second person trying to do first or third person's job. Don't give the facts to someone who already should know them!

Though it's tempting to try to give the audience facts by letting them eavesdrop on a conversation, be careful. You might end up with something as stilted and unnatural sounding as the little gem above. First person narrative would sound closer to what's really happening:

> I met her on a Saturday
> Her hair was wound in braids
> She walked up and she said hello
> And then she asked my name

Third person narrative is better too:

> He met her on a Saturday
> Her hair was wound in braids
> She walked up and she said hello
> And then she asked his name

Moving into first or third person narrative is one way to solve the problem. But sometimes you may be committed to second person. In that case, you have to find a way to make the conversation sound more natural. Do you really want the audience to know that it was Saturday and she had braids and she made the first move? If not, just drop the unnatural verse and write a better, more natural one. If the facts are important, you have to say them naturally, like you would in a real conversation:

> *I never felt anything quite as strong*
> as I did that Saturday night we met
> *You looked so fresh* with your hair in braids
> *And I felt like singing*
> When you walked right up and asked my name

By including personal information she couldn't have known, you've made the conversation more natural. Or this:

> *I still remember* the Saturday night we met
> Your hair so pretty, up in braids
> *You blew me away* when you said hello
> And asked me "What's your name?"

Both of these versions work because they include the singer's reactions to the facts. OK, so it's not great writing. Even so, it still sounds more natural, and once you know what approach to take, you can always polish up the language. The second version also includes the old "do you remember" ploy for introducing information. Put it in your own bag of tricks.

No matter the point of view, mothers will always have their modes of torment. This natural use of second person is maddenly effective. Any mother would be proud to use it.

The point is simple: Make second person conversational. If you want to give the audience a history lesson, either put it in third person or find a natural way to list your facts. If you gotta swing, make it quick and natural.

As a matter of habit, you should try out all three points of view, first, second and third person, for each lyric you write from now until you die, just to make sure you are using the best possible one for each song. Read your lyric aloud, each time substituting the different pronouns to see which you like best. Sometimes a change in point of view will raise a bland lyric from the dead.

Chapter Eleven

Point of View:
Second Person as Narrative

When you tell a story, it is usually narrative, either first person or third person. As we've seen, first person narrative includes the storyteller in the story, using first person and third person pronouns. Third person narrative uses only third person pronouns: he, she, it, they. There is no "I."

This Bob Seger lyric took me by surprise. It has all the qualities of a narrative, but uses Second Person, "you":

THE FIRE INSIDE
There's a hard moon risin' on the streets tonight
There's a reckless feeling in your heart as you head out tonight
Through the concrete canyons to the midtown lights
Where the latest neon promises are burning bright
Past the open windows on the darker streets
Where unseen angry voices flash and children cry
Past the phony posers with their worn out lines
The tired new money dressed to the nines
The lowlife dealers with their bad designs
And the dilettantes with their open minds
You're out on the town
Safe in the crowd
Ready to go for the ride
Searching the eyes
Looking for clues
There's no way you can hide
THE FIRE INSIDE

Well you've been to the clubs and the discotheques
Where they deal one another from the bottom of the deck of promises
Where the cautious loners and emotional wrecks
Do an acting stretch as a way to hide the obvious
And the lights go down and they dance real close
And for one brief instant they pretend they're safe and warm
Then the beat gets louder and the mood is gone
The darkness scatters as the lights flash on
They hold one another just a little too long
And they move apart and then move on
On to the street
On to the next
Safe in the knowledge that they tried
Faking the smile, hiding the pain
Never satisfied
THE FIRE INSIDE

Now the hour is late and he thinks you're asleep
And you listen to him dress and you listen to him leave like you knew
    he would
You hear his car pull away in the street
Then you move to the door and you lock it
When he's gone for good
Then you walk to the window
And you stare at the moon
Riding high and lonesome through the starlit sky
And it comes to you how it all slips away
Youth and beauty are gone one day
No matter what you dream or feel or say
It ends in dust and disarray
Like wind on the plains
Sand through the glass
Waves rolling in with the tide
Dreams die hard
And we watch them erode
But we cannot be denied
THE FIRE INSIDE

What's going on with Seger's use of second person? Second person is usually direct address—*I* talking to *you*. But there's no

I. Is *you* used as a substitute for first person? That's the way I sometimes talk to myself: "Come on Pat, can't you be clear for once?" instead of "I wish I could clear for once."

Try reading through the whole first verse in first person narrative:

> There's a hard moon risin' on the streets tonight
> *There's a reckless feeling in my heart as I head out tonight*
> Through the concrete canyons to the midtown lights
> Where the latest neon promises are burning bright
> Past the open windows on the darker streets
> Where unseen angry voices flash and children cry
> Past the phony posers with their worn out lines
> The tired new money dressed to the nines
> The lowlife dealers with their bad designs
> And the dilettantes with their open minds
> You're out on the town
> Safe in the crowd
> Ready to go for the ride
> Searching the eyes
> Looking for clues
> *There's no way I can hide*
> THE FIRE INSIDE

Clearly, Bob Seger is not using *you* as a disguise for *I.*

Continue until you finish the whole lyric. Of course, the pronouns have to change in verse three (at least with a Seger lead vocal):

> Now the hour is late and *she* thinks I'm asleep
> And I listen to *her* dress and I listen to *her* leave like I knew *she* would
> I hear *her* car pull away in the street
> Then I move to the door and I lock it
> When *she's* gone for good
> Then *I* walk to the window
> And *I* stare at the moon
> Riding high and lonesome through the starlit sky
> And it comes to *me* how it all slips away
> Youth and beauty are gone one day
> No matter what *I* dream or feel or say

It ends in dust and disarray
Like wind on the plains
Sand through the glass
Waves rolling in with the tide
Dreams die hard
And we watch them erode
But we cannot be denied
THE FIRE INSIDE

The result is a clear first person narrative. But something gets lost: a kind of universal feeling that "you" seems to add.

Let's try the lyric in third person:

There's a hard moon risin' on the streets tonight
There's a reckless feeling in *her* heart as *she* heads out tonight
Through the concrete canyons to the midtown lights
Where the latest neon promises are burning bright
Past the open windows on the darker streets
Where unseen angry voices flash and children cry
Past the phony posers with their worn out lines
The tired new money dressed to the nines
The lowlife dealers with their bad designs
And the dilettantes with their open minds
She's out on the town
Safe in the crowd
Ready to go for the ride
Searching the eyes
Looking for clues
There's no way she can hide
THE FIRE INSIDE

Continue reading the whole lyric in third person. Take your time. Now it's a clear third person narrative, landing squarely in storytelling mode.

Second person narrative serves up a tricky combination of third person narrative (where we watch the character) and direct address—talking right to the character. Part of it works like using "you" as a substitute for "one," as in "You get what you pay for = *One* gets what *one* pays for."

There's a hard moon risin' on the streets tonight
There's a reckless feeling in one's heart as one heads out tonight

Now stir in the illusion of direct address by using you instead of "one."

There's a hard moon risin' on the streets tonight
There's a reckless feeling in *your* heart as *you* head out tonight

Second person narrative actively forces us to say, "This character could easily be me." The universal theme set up in the lovely third verse helps too. One key to the lyric's success is the move to first person plural at the end:

And it comes to you how it all slips away
Youth and beauty are gone one day
No matter what you dream or feel or say
It ends in dust and disarray
Like wind on the plains
Sand through the glass
Waves rolling in with the tide
Dreams die hard
And *we* watch them erode
But *we* cannot be denied
THE FIRE INSIDE

We forces the listener into the emotion.

One test for second person narrative: Does it translate easily into third person? Try it with another second person narrative, Steeley Dan's *Kid Charlemagne*:

While the music played
You worked by candlelight
Those San Francisco nights
You were the best in town
Just by chance *you* crossed the diamond with the pearl
You turned it on the world
That's when *you* turned the world around

EXERCISE

Go ahead and translate it:

> While the music played
> *He* worked by candlelight . . .

Finish it.

EXERCISE

Translate it into first person narrative:

> While the music played
> *I* worked by candlelight . . .

Finish it. Each narrative mode makes you look at the lyric differently. Which do you like better for *Kid Charlemagne*? Yup. I like second person narrative best here too. But a cautionary note: Don't dash out and turn all your third person narratives into second person. Beware of the hangman: Don't tell facts to someone who should already know them!

You can also leave the narrative mode, using second person as a substitute for *I*, as in, "C'mon, can't you be clear for once?" Or as an internal command: "C'mon, be clear for once!" Leonard Cohen's *Dress Rehearsal Rag* is a good example. The character is standing in front of a mirror getting ready to shave:

> . . . Look at your body now, there's nothing much to save
> And a bitter voice in the mirror says "Hey Prince, you need a shave."
> Now, if you can manage to get your trembling fingers to behave
> Why don't you try unwrapping a stainless steel razor blade . . .
> . . . Cover up your face with soap, there, now you're Santa Claus
> and you've got an "A" for anyone who will give you his applause . . .

I suppose we could call it an internal monologue or dialogue. One thing is clear: narrative it ain't.

Practice with points of view. Get in the habit of checking *every lyric you write* from each POV. Sometimes a change will make all the difference. Mostly, you'll get your best results with direct address and with standard first and third person narratives. But don't let that keep you from checking out second person narrative. When it works, it works big time.

Chapter Twelve

Dialogue and Point of View

♪♪♪

Conversation overheard in a country home, using a surveillance microphone:

Alphonse: What gifts can I bring you to prove that my love for you is true? I want to make you mine forever. There's nothing on this earth I would not do.

Emma Rae: Anything I have wanted you have given willingly. So now there's only one more thing I need: If you love me give me wings. Don't be afraid if I fly. A bird in a cage will forget how to sing; if you love me give me wings.

Alphonse: (walking over to the window, staring into space) I just want to protect you, because this world is a dangerous place.

Emma Rae: (putting her arms around him) I know you mean well, but there's lessons I must learn for myself. If you love me give me wings. Don't be afraid if I fly. A bird in a cage will forget how to sing; if you trust me give me wings. Up above the clouds you can see forever, and I know you and I could learn to fly together. If you love me give me wings. Don't be afraid if I fly. A bird in a cage will forget how to sing; if you trust me give me wings. If you really love me give me wings.

Gosh, what a nice conversation. It even rhymes. How would you turn this dialogue into a song? Think about it for a minute. Go back, read it again, and try it.

No, it probably isn't a duet. Duets need equal characters, both of whom can say the same chorus. Emma Rae is the only one here who can say "Give me wings." Unless you're writing opera (sung dialogue), you're better off having one singer tell us about the conversation, complete with quotes. The real trick is selecting a point of view to set the whole thing up.

Here are your options:

1. FIRST PERSON NARRATIVE

> I asked her, "What gifts can I bring you
> To prove that my love for you is true?"

or,

> He asked me, "What gifts can I bring you
> To prove that my love for you is true?"

In first person narrative the singer tells us about a conversation he/she actually had with some third party. Like someone coming into work and saying, "Guess who I talked to yesterday. You'll never believe who he was with!" And then telling you the story.

2. DIRECT ADDRESS

> I asked you, "What gifts can I bring you
> To prove that my love for you is true?"

In direct address either the singer is talking directly to us, or else to some unseen you. We're watching him/her have a conversation with a second person.

3. THIRD PERSON NARRATIVE

> He asked her, "What gifts can I bring you
> To prove that my love for you is true"

Now our singer is a storyteller, pointing to a scene in the distance. The singer isn't in the story, and neither are we.

Let's try all three.

First Person Narrative

> I asked her, "What gifts can I bring you
> To prove that my love for you is true?

Want to make you mine forever.
There's nothing on this earth I would not do."

She said, "Anything I have wanted
You have given willingly.
So now there's only one more thing I need.

If you love me Give Me Wings
Don't be afraid if I fly
A bird in a cage will forget how to sing
If you love me Give Me Wings"

I walked over to the window
Silently stared into space
And said, "I just want to protect you.
Cause this world is a dangerous place."

She put her arms around me
She said "I know you mean well,
But there's lessons I must learn for myself

If you love me Give Me Wings
Don't be afraid if I fly
A bird in a cage will forget how to sing
If you trust me Give Me Wings"
She said, "Up above the clouds you can see forever
And I know you and I could learn to fly together

If you love me Give Me Wings
Don't be afraid if I fly
A bird in a cage will forget how to sing
If you trust me Give Me Wings
If you really love me Give Me Wings."

The point of view works OK, but something is askew. The emotion feels off balance, a little forced. Why is this guy standing up there with his microphone telling us the story, anyway? What's his point?

Maybe the source of the problem is that the lyric is about her, not I. Our first version of first person narrative shines the spotlight on the wrong person. In order for the male character to sing the song, he'd have to have something important to say about the story at the end, like Schlitz's *The Gambler:* In his final words I found and ace that I could keep. Maybe something like: I gave her her freedom and we've been great ever since/ Soaring together, lovers and friends.

So let's try it the other way. Since it is her story, maybe she should be the narrator:

> He asked me, "What gifts can I bring you
> To prove that my love for you is true?
> Want to make you mine forever.
> There's nothing on this earth I would not do."
>
> I said, "Anything I have wanted
> You have given willingly.
> So now there's only one more thing I need.
>
> If you love me Give Me Wings
> Don't be afraid if I fly
> A bird in a cage will forget how to sing
> If you love me Give Me Wings."

Go back to the first version and make the rest of the changes.

This point of view is better, but not terrific. Again, why is she raising the microphone and telling us these facts? We'd still need something like: He gave me my freedom and we've been great ever since/Soaring together, lovers and friends.

Moral: If the singer is the *I* in a story, you've got to give him/ her a good reason for telling it.

Direct Address

Next let's get up close and personal:

> I asked you, "What gifts can I bring you
> To prove that my love for you is true?
> Want to make you mine forever.
> There's nothing on this earth I would not do."
>
> You said, "Anything I have wanted

You have given willingly.
So now there's only one more thing I need.

If you love me Give Me Wings
Don't be afraid if I fly
A bird in a cage will forget how to sing
If you love me Give Me Wings"

I walked over to the window
Silently stared into space
I said, "I just want to protect you.
Cause this world is a dangerous place."

You put your arms around me
Said, "I know you mean well,
But there's lessons I must learn for myself

If you love me Give Me Wings . . ."

Total disaster—the worst of history lessons. You was already there during the conversation, so what's the point of telling her about it again? The same is true if the woman sings the song:

You asked me, "What gifts can I bring you
To prove that my love for you is true?"

As we saw two chapters ago (second person and the hang-man), telling someone what they already know doesn't make for credible dialogue.

Third Person Narrative

Finally, look at the point of view of the actual lyric by Don Schlitz and Rhonda Kye Fleming.

GIVE ME WINGS

He asked her "What gifts can I bring you
To prove that my love for you is true?
Want to make you mine forever.
There's nothing on this earth I would not do."

She said, "Anything I have wanted
You have given willingly.
So now there's only one more thing I need.

If you love me Give Me Wings
Don't be afraid if I fly
A bird in a cage will forget how to sing
If you love me Give Me Wings."

He walked over to the window
Silently stared into space
He said, "I just want to protect you.
Cause this world is a dangerous place."

She put her arms around him
She said, "I know you mean well,
But there's lessons I must learn for myself

If you love me Give Me Wings
Don't be afraid if I fly
A bird in a cage will forget how to sing
If you trust me Give Me Wings."

She said, "Up above the clouds you can see forever
And I know you and I could learn to fly together

If you love me Give Me Wings
Don't be afraid if I fly
A bird in a cage will forget how to sing
If you trust me Give Me Wings
If you really love me Give Me Wings."

Nifty. It doesn't matter if the singer is male or female, the dialogue seems complete and natural. Not that third person narrative is always the right answer for every lyric that uses dialogue. You should read every lyric you write in each point of view. See how each one feels, then decide which one works best.

Something on structure while we're here.

There's more to like about this little gem, so while we're here, let's take a quick look at its structure, a really nice display of technical savvy.

The verses are fairly balanced—four lines in common meter, rhyming xaxa.

	rhyme	stresses
He asked her "What gifts can I bring you	x	3+
To prove that my love for you is true?	a	3
Want to make you mine forever.	x	3+
There's nothing on this earth I would not do."	a	3

Pretty standard stuff. But beware, it's a setup to lull you into a false sense of security.

The section between the verse and chorus (call it whatever you want to: vest, pre-chorus, prime, lift, channel, runway, climb—I call it a transitional bridge) throws us off balance with its three lines:

> She said, "Anything I have wanted
> You have given willingly.
> So now there's only one more thing I need"

Or, if you like, two lines of wickedly unequal length:

> She said, "Anything I have wanted you have given willingly.
> So now there's only one more thing I need"

We are toppled into the chorus, praying to find a secure landing. Perfect. That's what a transitional bridge is supposed to do.

Once we're securely into the chorus, things seem OK. The first two lines feel sturdy, balancing each other with 3-stresses:

> If you love me give me wings
> Don't be afraid if I fly

Then a four-stress line sets up a little more tension:

> A bird in a cage will forget how to sing

Boy, do we ever want a 3-stress line rhyming with "fly." How come? The aba rhyme scheme, Wings/fly/sing begs for a pairing with the unrhymed word. What do you want to hear? Maybe something like

If you love me give me wings
Don't be afraid if I fly
A bird in a cage will forget how to sing
I must soar beyond the sky

OK, my line is pretty cheesy, but even so, it does the job, resolving the tension nicely, both structurally and emotionally. The rhyme structure, wings/fly/sing/sky, feels much more resolved than the situation of the song intends: she's asking for, not getting, wings. . . . That's why the real chorus' rhyme scheme, abaa, is so perfect.

If you love me give me wings
Don't be afraid if I fly
A bird in a cage will forget how to sing
If you love me give me wings

The last line fools you (I call it a deceptive cadence), and in doing so, accomplishes three things: 1) it repeats the title—a good commercial move; 2) the structural surprise spotlights the title; 3) it resolves the chorus, though not as solidly as a rhyme for "fly" would have. The surprise rhyme is emotionally better suited to the intent of the chorus since it's a little less secure.

Neat structure. It lights up the title and supports the emotion of the lines with perfect prosody. I'm glad we looked.

Chapter Thirteen

Meter:
Something in Common

The sea captain of western popular music is the eight-bar musical section, subdivided into two-and four-bar units. Expressed in quarter notes, old salty looks like this:

The eight-bar system is really one piece. Each of the subdivisions is a landmark along the voyage, giving directions and charting relationships. The end of bar two rests:

Then we tack into bars three and four:

—what a different trip this section is (probably headed into the wind). Though we're at the end of four bars, we certainly feel unbalanced, and must continue:

That's better: familiar territory. Not only that, but we know exactly what to expect next: Because of the match between bars one and two and bars five and six, we expect bars seven and eight to match bars three and four. When they do, we have arrived at the end of the trip. We feel balanced:

Of course, this has been a very simple trip, but you'd be surprised how basic it is to western music, from Bach to Berry. Go back and take another look at the complete thing, and, while you're at it, mark the strong and weak notes in each two-bar group.

DUM da DUM da DUM da DUM	4 stresses
DUM da DUM da DUM	3 stresses
DUM da DUM da DUM da DUM	4 stresses
DUM da DUM da DUM	3 stresses

The continuous voyage is organized according to a very simple principle: Longer/Shorter/Longer/Shorter.

You can't stop until you get to port. Now look at this simple nursery rhyme:

Máry hád a líttle lámb	4 stresses
Its fléece was whíte as snów	3 stresses
And éverywhére that Máry wént	4 stresses
The lámb was súre to gó	3 stresses

Yup, it has something in common with the voyage we just took:

DUM da DUM da DUM da DUM	4 stresses
DUM da DUM da DUM	3 stresses
DUM da DUM da DUM da DUM	4 stresses
DUM da DUM da DUM	3 stresses

Like the eight-bar unit, this meter is the staple of songwriters from the early troubadours to Tom Waits. It is even called common meter, partly because of its pervasiveness (the basis of nursery rhymes—e.g., *Mary Mary, Quite Contrary . . . Old Mother Hubbard . . .*), partly because of its relationship to musical form. Imagine our old seafarer singing:

O Western Wind, when wilt thou blow	4 stresses
The small rain down can rain?	3 stresses
Christ, that my love were in my arms	4 stresses
And I in my bed again	3 stresses

Since common meter is based on strong stresses, it doesn't really matter where the unstressed syllables fall. Like this:

If Máry hád a líttle lámb	4 stresses
Whose fléece was as whíte as snów	3 stresses
Then éverywhére Máry wént	4 stresses
The lámb would be súre to gó	3 stresses

or even this:

It was Máry who hád the líttlest lámb	4 stresses
With fléece just as whíte as the snów	3 stresses
O and éverywhére that Máry might chánce	4 stresses
The lámb would most súrely gó	3 stresses

Sometimes common meter omits a strong stress. The most usual variation shortens the four-stress lines to three stresses, plus an unstressed syllable at the end:

Sátan rídes the fréeway	3 + stresses
Pláying róck and róll	3 stresses
Gíve him lánes of léeway	3 + stresses
He lóngs to dríve your sóul	3 stresses

It still works the same way: Longer/Shorter/Longer/Shorter.

The important point is that the first and second phrases don't match: three-plus stresses is still longer than three stresses.

Sometimes a strong stress isn't really that strong:

I heard a fly buzz when I died	4 stresses (2 adjacent)
The stillness in the room	2 stresses (*in* is pretty wimpy)
Was like the stillness in the air	4 stresses (2 of which are pretty wimpy)
Between the heaves of storm	3 stresses
—Emily Dickinson	

Common meter is nothing if not flexible. Sometimes the four-stress lines divide into two phrases. Sometimes the four-stress and three-stress lines add up to one complete phrase. Here, in one verse (written in triple meter), are both events:

They might 'a split up or they might 'a capsized	2 phrases, each 2 stresses
They might have broke deep and took water	
And all that remains is the faces and names	
Of the wives and the sons and the daughters	2 lines equal one phrase of 7 stresses
Gordon Lightfoot—*The Wreck of the Edmund Fitzgerald*	

Common meter is a great starting point for creating a lyric, *and* for assuring a musical match. But remember, I said *starting point.* Writing in common meter is not a *goal*, it is a *tool*. Since common meter creates expectations, you can learn to create nice little surprises. Watch Paul Simon work his magic in these two lovely unbalanced bridges:

First, from *Still Crazy After All These Years*

Foúr in the mórning, crápped out, yáwning	4 stresses
Lónging my lífe awáy	3 stresses
I'll never worŕy, whý should Í	4 stresses
It's aíl gonna fáde	2 stresses (unbalancing)

The short ending leaves us hanging, supporting the emotion

of the bridge. (What? Structure can be used to support emotion? Yup. Structure can be used to support emotion.)

Next, from *Train in the Distance*:

Twó disappoińted beliévers	3 + stresses
Twó people pláying the gaḿe	3 stresses (*people* set on weak beats)
Negótiátions and lovésongs	3 + stresses (*songs* is weak in *lovesongs*)
Are óften mistáken for ońe and the saḿe	4 stresses

The last line unbalances the section and turns spotlights onto the idea. A neat but effective ploy: If you want people to notice something, put it in spotlights. Ergo, put your important ideas in spotlights. Corollary: Don't turn on spotlights just to be cute.

Learn to cram your ideas into alternating four-stress and three-stress phrases. If they resist, let them, and see whether the results create any nifty little surprises, especially if the surprises help the meaning. The exercise will do you good; it will help you chart your course more clearly, in stages that are foreseeable and easy to accomplish. If you need to take a detour, you will know where you are when you leave, and it will help you keep safely under control. A simple detour:

You've never felt what lonely is	4 stresses
Till you've flown the night alone	3 stresses
And the wind has blown you almost to despair	5 stresses
The sky runs black as midnight	3 + stresses
And the strip is hard to see	3 stresses
HEADED INTO CHARLOTTE ON A PRAYER	5 stresses

Organizing your ideas into common meter may take a little work, but probably not that much, since, with *Old King Cole* and *Little Miss Muffett*, it is ingrained from your earliest childhood. Any ideas—a telemarketing call:

> I had to call to say hello
> I hope you're gonna buy
> Times are tough and rent is due
> And I've got songs to write

Deciding whether to call for a date:

> I wanna call, I wanna call
> But I know I'll sound too scared
> My self-esteem is plunging fast
> O do I do I dare?

EXERCISE

Even your grocery list. (Your turn. Try doing one in duples—da Dum da Dum— and one in triples—da da Dum da da Dum.

Learn to think in common meter. It will give you plenty in common with every Billboard chart in history, and plenty in common with the language of song from its earliest chartings. You will be sailing through it and its variations as long as you write lyrics. It's a strong map to work from; it will help you chart a manageable course to keep you from getting lost when those prosodic zigs and zags take you into lovely and unexpected waters.

Chapter Fourteen

Meter:
Two By Two

A s we saw in the last chapter, common meter typically organizes music into a single eight-bar unit, running (two bars + two bars) + (two bars + two bars). The second line of common meter, comprising bars three and four, contains only three stresses, keeping the entire system moving until it is matched at line four (bars seven and eight).

When you want to organize into four-bar units rather than eight-bar units, all you have to do is match bars one and two with bars three and four. Here's the paradigm:

Eénie Méenie Míney Móe	4 stresses
Cátch a Tíger ón the tóe	4 stresses
íf he hóllers máke him páy	4 stresses
Fífty dóllars évery dáy	4 stresses

The lines are four-stress balanced lines called *couplets*. They move differently. There's no problem stopping after line two:

Eénie Méenie Míney Móe	4 stresses
Cátch a Tíger ón the tóe	4 stresses

Not so with Common meter:

Máry hád a líttle lámb	4 stresses
Fléece as whíte as snów	3 stresses

Common meter gives us an I.O.U., while the matched phrases of couplets let us stop for lunch and a quick nap. Here's a real one:

The tíme you wón your tówn the ráce
We cháired you thróugh the márket pláce
Mán and bóy stood chéering by
And hóme we bróught you shóulder hígh
    A.E. Housman—To an Athlete Dying Young

USING COUPLETS

Couplets usually rhyme, marking stopping places for the ear. They form a lyrical and musical unit, typically four bars long. They move us forward in regular, balanced steps with four stressed notes in each two-bar section.

You can easily extend from four lines to six without getting too far off balance. Look at the first verse of *Where've You Been,* by Don Henry and Jon Vesner:

Claire had all but given up
When she and Edwin fell in love
She touched his face and shook her head
In disbelief she finally said
In many dreams I've held you near
Now at last you're finally here

The feeling is slightly unstable, since we have an odd number of couplets, yet an even number of lines, a subtle and interesting verse structure. You can use it to create a strong sense of center, yet raise expectations that something else is coming.

You can also use a couplet at the end of a section of common meter for acceleration and contrast:

> Claire had all but given up
> Then fell in love with Ed
> She touched his face and closed her eyes
> In disbelief she said
> In many dreams I've held you near
> Now at last you're finally here

The ending couplet creates a real sense of interest and arrival.

You can use couplets to set up an expectation of balance, then take a different route. This from David Wilcox's *Eye of the Hurricane:*

Tank is full, switch is on	4 stresses
Night is warm, cops are gone	4 stresses
Rocket bike is all her own	4 stresses
It's called a Hurricane	3 stresses
She told me once it's quite a ride	4 stresses
It's shaped so there's this place inside	4 stresses
Where, if you're moving you can hide	4 stresses
Safe within the rain	3 stresses

Neat structure! The odd fourth line stands out because we expected a four-stress rhymed couplet. Instead, we get a three-stress unrhymed line, handing us an I.O.U. that isn't cashed in until line eight. It's a good way to create a seamless eight-line (sixteen-bar) section.

WITHOUT COUPLETS

What happens when four-stress lines aren't rhymed in couplets? Look at this section of *The End of the Innocence* by Don Henley and Bruce Hornsby:

Remember when the days were long	4 stresses
And rolled beneath a deep blue sky	4 stresses
Didn't have a care in the world	4 stresses

With mommy and daddy standin' by	4 stresses

This is a more leisurely trip, with balanced four-bar phrases that settle gently, rather than asking for forward motion. After we've seen only the first two lines,

Remember when the days were long	4 stresses
And rolled beneath a deep blue sky	4 stresses

there is no urgent push forward, as there would have been if the lines were unmatched.

Mary had a little lamb	4 stresses
Whose fleece was white as snow	3 stresses

pushes forward, while the four-stress couplets don't:

Mary had a little lamb	4 stresses
Whose fleece was white as deepest snow	4 stresses

Instead we just roll smoothly along, in no particular hurry.

	rhyme scheme	
Remember when the days were long	×	4 stresses
And rolled beneath a deep blue sky	a	4 stresses
Didn't have a care in the world	×	4 stresses
With mommy and daddy standin' by	a	4 stresses

When the next three lines come along in rhyme, we can feel the acceleration, a strong pressure building forward:

But "happily ever after" fails	b	4 stresses
And we've been poisoned by these fairy tales	b	4 stresses
The lawyers dwell on small details	b	4 stresses
Since daddy had to fly	c	3 stresses

Seven four-stress lines in a row, and after three rhymed lines in a row, an unrhymed 3-stress line! It's a huge I.O.U. that you can actually hear being cashed in sixteen lines later, after a pre-chorus, a chorus and the entire second verse have come in between. That's the power of the expectations these balanced lines are able to create.

It's interesting that the last line of the verse, "Since daddy had to fly," sounds unrhymed. It should rhyme with *sky* and *by* in lines two and four, but since the first four lines close off to form a unit, we won't hear the connection.

The next four lines move into common meter. After all the four stress couplets in the verse, the contrast is startling:

	rhyme scheme	
But I know a place where we can go	x	4 stresses
That's still untouched by men	d	3 stresses
We'll sit and watch the clouds roll by	x	4 stresses
And the tall grass wave in the wind	d	3 stresses

The section moves in a completely different way— in a four-line unit rather than two by two. We get a simultaneous effect of speeding up (with shorter second and fourth lines), and slowing down (less frequent rhymes). It's a great contrast to use for this transitional section (or prechorus), preparing us to go back to four stress lines:

	rhyme scheme	
You can lay your head back on the ground	a	4 stresses
And let your hair fall all around me	a	4 stresses
Offer up your best defense	b	4 stresses
But this is the end	b	2 stresses
This is *The End of the Innocence*	b	4 stresses

All the mixing and matching of four-stress couplets and common meter has led to this chorus. Here's the payoff for all the balanced lines and even numbers of bars. With a maddeningly simple move of inserting only a piece of the last line, "But this is the end," everything is thrown off balance. There are now an odd number of lines in the chorus. There is an odd rhyme scheme. There is a two-stress line for the first time. And the chorus stretches beyond the eight-bar units we saw in the verse and prechorus into eleven bars. An effective way to showcase the title. This is *The End of the Innocence*.

Throwing it off balance keeps it from closing solidly, supporting the emotion of the idea—a sort of bittersweet longing that feels a little airy and suspended, matching the structural asymmetry perfectly. Very impressive. And all done in couplets and common meter.

EXERCISE

Here are a few exercises to get you moving. Write a section for each of these models and watch it in action. Then put a few of the more unusual rhyme schemes in your tool box for later use. Offer your listener some nice surprises.

		rhyme scheme			rhyme scheme
1.	4 stresses	a	2.	4 stresses	a
	4 stresses	a		4 stresses	a
	4 stresses	b		4 stresses	a
	4 stresses	b		4 stresses	a

		rhyme scheme			rhyme scheme
3.	4 stresses	a	4.	4 stresses	a
	4 stresses	a		3 stresses	b
	4 stresses	b		4 stresses	c
	4 stresses	a		4 stresses	b

		rhyme scheme			rhyme scheme
5.	4 stresses	a	6.	4 stresses	a
	3 stresses	b		3 stresses	b
	4 stresses	c		4 stresses	a
	4 stresses	c		4 stresses	a

		rhyme scheme			rhyme scheme
7.	4 stresses	a	8.	4 stresses	a
	3 stresses	b		4 stresses	a
	4 stresses	a		4 stresses	a

3 stresses	b
4 stresses	c
4 stresses	c

3 stresses	b
4 stresses	c
4 stresses	c
4 stresses	c
3 stresses	b

	rhyme scheme
9. 4 stresses	a
4 stresses	b
4 stresses	a
4 stresses	b
4 stresses	c
4 stresses	c
4 stresses	c
4 stresses	c

Pretty easy stuff, step by step. But you can build interesting structures by mixing and matching couplets and common meter. Obviously, Horatio, there are more lines available in the universe than are found in these two philosophies, but they, with their combinations and variations, can take us a long way without stopping anywhere else.

Chapter Fifteen

Form Follows Function
Building the Perfect Beast

O hMyGod Artie, stop!" yells Herbie. Artie's '69 VW microbus wobbles over to the side of the road, next to a cream-and-baby-blue Maserati convertible parked in the lot. "Boy, I'd like to drive that beauty. Looks like it really flies." "Whew," whistles Artie, "look at it—low, wide wheel base, scooped front, rear foil. Definitely built for speed." A physicist or aeronautical engineer could give a more precise description, but Artie and Herbie have it nailed anyway. As much as they love Artie's microbus, they know it won't win any races, because it isn't built for speed. But that Maserati sure could. Intuitively, they apply the principle *form follows function*. If you asked them the right questions, they'd be able to describe the two ways this principle works:

1. When you look at an individual car, you can figure out what it's built to do (function) by its design (form). Conversely, when you build a car, you figure out its design by what you want it to do. If you want a race car, build it heavy, wide and lower in front than in back so the wind will press it to the track. If you want an economy car, build it light and shape it to cut wind resistance. This is called the principle of prosody.

2. When you look at two cars, you see whether they're different or the same. When they're the same design, they should have the same function. When they have different designs, they should have different functions. This is the principle of contrast.

It doesn't matter whether we're talking about cars, rhyme schemes, architecture, or lyrics.

PROSODY

Prosody (prahz-a-dee) means that elements are working together for a common purpose, for example, when we line up words and notes—matching stressed notes appropriately with stressed syllables. Or when we relate shape to speed in designing racing cars. We could create a relationship between rhythm and meaning by writing about galloping horses in a clippity-clop rhythm.

> The Assýrian came dówn like the wólf on the fóld
> And his cóhorts were gléaming in sílver and góld
> —Byron

We could also write about difficult deeds by using strings of stressed syllables to slow the rhythm down:

> When Ajáx strives sóme róck's vást wéight to thrów
> The líne tóo lábors, and the wórds móve slów
> —Pope

As a writer, you'll usually look from a car designer's perspective—from function to form. You know what you want to say, so you have to design form to support your ideas.

Your tools for designing your lyric's shapes are phrase lengths, rhythms and rhyme schemes. For example, say there's a place in your verse where emotion gets pretty active or intense. You might try putting rhymes (both phrase-end and internal rhyme) close together, and try using short phrases. Like this:

1.	You can't play Ping-Pong with my heart	a
	You dominate the table	b
	My nerves are shot, you've won the set	c
	Your curves have got me in a sweat	c
	My vision's blurred, can't see the net	c
	I'm feeling most unstable	b

Built for speed. Consecutive rhymes "set/net/sweat" slam the ideas home. The internal rhymes "nerves/curves/blurred" and "shot/got" put us in overdrive. The acceleration creates prosody: the mutual support of structure and meaning—form follows function.

What would the ride feel like if we toned down the rhyme action?

2.	You can't play Ping-Pong with my heart	a
	You dominate the table	b
	My nerves are shot, I've come apart	a
	You wink and smile, still feeling playful	b
	Weak and numb, I miss the mark	a
	Feeling most unstable	b

Out pops the rear parachute. Prosody evaporates, or at least diminishes when the rhymes are spread out into a regular pattern. But the short phrases in lines three, four and five still press on the accelerator. If we lengthen some of the shorter phrases, we let off the gas even more.

3.	You can't play Ping-Pong with my heart	a
	You dominate the table	b
	My nerves are shot, you've won the point	x
	Your slams have put me in a sweat	x
	My vision's weak, can't see the ball	x
	I'm feeling most unstable	b

Now the structure acts more like a slow-moving '68 VW microbus, while the meaning still dreams of checkered flags on the Grand Prix Circuit. Bad combination.

EXERCISE

We might as well destroy prosody completely while we're at it. This time, you do it. Rewrite below so lines three and five contain one long phrase each, instead of two shorter ones. Be careful not to rhyme.

3.	You can't play Ping-Pong with my heart	a
	You dominate the table	b
	. . .	x
	Your slams have put me in a sweat	x
	. . .	x
	I'm feeling most unstable	b

Compare your result to the original and you will see what an important role structure can play in support of meaning. If you're careful how you build your form, you can make it work for you. Tend to the prosody of form and function, and your structure will become a powerful and expressive ally rather than an obstacle standing between you and what you really meant to say.

THE PRINCIPLE OF CONTRAST

Herbie and Artie know the difference between their microbus and the cream-and-baby-blue Maserati. No big mystery—they're built different. This is another way to look at "form follows function." Simple logic: Things that look the same should do the same thing. Things that look different should do different things. A microbus is not a Maserati.

Verses in a song should all have the same function—they develop the plot, characters, or situations of the song. That's why they're all called verses. Because the verses all have the same function, they should all have the same form. Easy, huh?

Or this: When you move from a verse to another function, for example, to a chorus function (commentary, summary), the form should change—the rhyme scheme, phrase lengths, number of phrases, or rhythms of phrases. Maybe all four.

Form follows function is the real rationale behind what often look like silly rules:

> All verses should have the same rhyme scheme!
> Change the rhyme scheme when you get to the chorus

Look at this verse and its chorus:

SOUTHERN COMFORT

Verse 1
> Spanish moss hanging low
> Swaying from the trees
> Honeysuckle, sweet magnolia
> Riding on the breeze
> Southern evenings, southern stars
> Used to bring me peace
> But now they only make me cry
> They only make me realize

Chorus

> There's no SOUTHERN COMFORT
> Unless you're in my arms
> You're the only cure
> For this aching in my heart
> I've searched everywhere
> Tried the bedrooms, tried the bars
> But there's no SOUTHERN COMFORT
> Unless you're in my arms

Each section contains, roughly, the same number of phrases. No contrast there.

The verse rhymes its alternate lines, except at the end, where it accelerates with a couplet. The chorus rhymes every other line too, without the couplet acceleration at the end:

Verse		**Chorus**	
low	x	comfort	x
trees	a	arms	a
magnolia	x	cure	x
breeze	a	heart	a
stars	x	where	x
peace	a	bars	a
cry	b	comfort	x
realize	b	arms	a

Still not much contrast between the sections. The verse contains two complete sections of common meter rhythm. The only variation is the extra stressed syllable in the last line.

	# stresses
Spánish móss hánging lów	4
Swáying fróm the treés	3
Hóneysúckle, sweét magnólia	4
Ríding ón the breéze	3
Soúthern évenings, soúthern stárs	4
úsed to bríng me peáce	3
But nów they ónly máke me cry	4
They ónly máke me réalizé	4

That's a lot of common meter, but there's more. Look at the chorus.

	# stresses
There's nó SOÚTHERN CÓMFORT	3 +
Unléss you're ín my árms	3
Yoú're the ónly cúre	3
For this áching ín my heárt	3
I've seárched éverywhére	3
Triéd the bédrooms, triéd the bárs	4
But there's nó SOÚTHERN CÓMFORT	3 +
Unléss you're ín my árms	3

Although most of the phrases have three stresses, the section still leans toward common meter:

1. The balancing phrases are three stresses, the signature length of common meter.

2. The opening phrase is longer than three stresses, three plus— a normal variation of common meter's four-stress line. When you want two sections to contrast, the opening phrase of the new section must make a difference immediately. If you don't make a difference there, don't bother.

3. The two three-stress phrases with extra weak syllables are in the same positions as four-stress phrases in common meter, leaving only two contrasting phrases in the entire chorus. And they're the same length as half the lines in the verse.

Essentially, by the time we finish the chorus, we have been through four common meter systems. That's a lot. Imagine the boredom by the time you finish four more:

Verse 2
> Tried my best to ease the hurt
> Leave the pain behind
> Evenings sitting on the porch
> You're always on my mind
> SOUTHERN COMFORT after dark
> Helps me face the night
> But there's nothing to look forward to
> 'Cept looking back to loving you

Chorus
> There's no SOUTHERN COMFORT

Unless you're in my arms
You're the only cure
For this aching in my heart
I've searched everywhere
Tried the bedrooms, tried the bars
But there's no SOUTHERN COMFORT
Unless you're in my arms

Ho-hum structure. If the lyric's meaning were more interesting, there might be some hope, but it's not that interesting. Even if the meaning shone in eleven shades of microbus Day-Glo, the structure still should help the meaning, not hurt it.

The bridge finally delivers a contrast, but by then everyone has wandered off for a hot dog. It's too late.

Bar to bar
Face to face
Someone new takes your place
No one's ever new
I always turn them into you

Then two more lumps of common meter for the tombstone:

Chorus
There's no SOUTHERN COMFORT
Unless you're in my arms
You're the only cure
For this aching in my heart
I've searched everywhere
Tried the bedrooms, tried the bars
But there's no SOUTHERN COMFORT
Unless you're in my arms

EXERCISE

As an exercise, try to design a verse that contrasts with the chorus. You might look at Jim Rushing's *Slow Healing Heart*, or Janis Ian's *Some People's Lives* as a way of handling eight-line structures. Alternately, you might try unbalancing the structure by shortening it.

Try it before you read further.

The rewrite below balances six lines against two rather than dividing the verse into two four-line sections of common meter.

	rhyme	stress
Spánish móss hánging lów	x	4
Bówing fróm the trées	a	3
Hóneysúckle ríding ón the bréeze	a	5
Sóuthern évenings, sóuthern stárs	x	4
Swéet magnólia níghts	x	3
Uséd to bring me hármony and péace	a	5
Látely théy just máke me cry	b	4
They ónly máke me realíze	b	4

Chorus

> There's no SOUTHERN COMFORT
> Unless you're in my arms
> You're the only cure
> For this aching in my heart
> I've searched everywhere
> Tried the bedrooms, tried the bars
> But there's no SOUTHERN COMFORT
> Unless you're in my arms

Now the verse and chorus look different. Even Artie would notice. Though this lyric could still use major rewriting, at least its structure isn't stuck in the mud.

Prosody and Contrast

Of course, contrast between sections can also add prosody:

Verse:	If I went into analysis	a
	And took myself apart	b
	And laid me out for both of us to see	c
	You'd go into paralysis	a

	Right there in my arms	b
	Finding out you're not a bit like me	c
Chorus:	READY OR NOT	d
	We've got what we've got	d
	Let's give it a shot	d
	READY OR NOT	d

The chorus really zips along by changing to short phrases and consecutive rhymes. The speed is really a result of contrast: it seems so fast only because the verse has been so leisurely. Both Paul Simon's *Fifty Ways to Leave Your Lover* and Beth Nielsen Chapman's *Years* work on the same principle. Here's the first verse and chorus from *Years*.

	# stresses (w/musical setting)
I went home for Christmas to the house that I grew up in	6
Going home was something after all those years	5
I drove up Monterey Street and I felt a little sadness	6
When I turned left on Laurel and the house appeared	5
And I snuck up to that rocking chair	
where the winter sunlight slanted on the screened in porch	9
And I looked out past the shade tree	
that my laughing daddy planted on the day that I was born	9

Chorus	And I let time go by so slow	3
	And I made every moment last	3
	And I thought about YEARS	2
	How they take so long	2
	And they go so fast	2

The verse lines are lingering and relaxed just like the daughter. The chorus shows how fast years go by, accelerating the pace with shorter phrases. Not only is there contrast, but the contrast supports the meaning. Even within the chorus, the longer phrases slow time down; shorter phrases step on the accelerator:

Chorus	And I let time go by so slow	3
	And I made every moment last	3
	And I thought about YEARS	2

| How they take so long | 2 |
| And they go so fast | 2 |

Beth Nielsen Chapman sets the first two lines into four bars of music. The last three also fit into four bars, but the last line, "And they go so fast" is only one bar, supporting the lyric prosody perfectly. Nice stuff.

Become a designer: Fit form to function. When you run with the LA fast-track set, step out with the Maserati. But when you want to join Artie and Herbie for the next Dead concert, go in style in the Day-Glo microbus. Stop to consider what you need, and then build it. Have an effective, interesting structure ready for any occasion.

Chapter Sixteen

The Great Balancing Act

Courting Danger on the High Wire

♪ ♪ ♪

I magine a high-wire artist at the circus. There she is, arms extended, stepping ever so carefully along the thin wire. Step. Wobble . . . (gasps from the crowd!) Steadies herself. (audible relief.) Step. Ooops. Step . . . No doubt she could move smoothly and quickly across, but she is making (or barely making) her aerial journey for our pleasure and excitement. She plays with our emotions knowing we will remember her trip long after the lights and noise fade to nothing.

Writing lyrics is a high-wire act: the way you keep or lose your balance makes all the difference to your audience. Sometimes a little aerial drama may be just what you need to get and keep your listener's undivided attention.

Here's a very simple balancing (or unbalancing) technique: Control the number of phrases in your sections and you can learn to keep or lose your balance in just the right places, while gasps and cheers attend your every move.

In general, assuming that phrase lengths are more or less equal, and the rhyme scheme moves more or less evenly, an even number of phrases creates a balanced section; an odd number, an unbalanced section. The simplest case is repetition. An even number of phrases balances this section:

Baby can you feel it
Baby can you feel it,

While an odd number:

> Baby can you feel it
> Baby can you feel it
> Baby can you feel it

unbalances it. Not a hard concept, but a very useful one. You can get the same effect without repetition. Like this three-phrase section:

> How am I to reach you
> When am I to touch you
> How am I to hold you.

Common meter pairs off its longer second and fourth phrases and its shorter first and third:

> Mary had a little lamb
> Its fleece was white as snow
> Everywhere that Mary went
> The lamb was sure to go.

In this next one, the two short phrases of the third line add up to equal the first phrase, giving us another balanced piece of common meter like *Mary Had a Little Lamb*:

> Yes I'm THE GREAT PRETENDER
> Pretending that I'm doing well
> My need is such, I pretend too much
> I'm lonely but no one can tell

But if we trim it to three phrases, it unbalances:

> O yes I'm THE GREAT PRETENDER
> Pretending that I'm doing well
> I'm lonely but no one can tell

How do we *use* balancing and unbalancing? Stated simply, unbalanced sections make you want to move to find a stable spot. Balanced sections stop motion. They pause for a rest. Balancing and unbalancing a lyric in the right places gives you at least four audience-grabbing strategies: (1) spotlighting important ideas; (2) pushing one section forward into another section; (3) contrasting one section with another one; (4) setting up a need for a balancing section or phrase.

Watch the high-wire work of Janis Ian and Kye Fleming, in this lovely lyric, from Janis' album, *Breaking Silence*:

SOME PEOPLE'S LIVES

		rhyme scheme
Verse 1	Some people's lives	a
	Run down like clocks	b
	One day they stop	b
	That's all they've got	b
Verse 2	Some lives wear out	a
	Like old tennis shoes	b
	No one can use	b
	It's sad but it's true	b
Chorus 1	Didn't anybody tell them	x
	Didn't anybody see	a
	Didn't anybody love them	x
	Like you love me?	a
Verse 3	Some people's eyes	a
	Fade like their dreams	b
	Too tired to rise	a
	Too tired to sleep	b
Verse 4	Some people laugh	a
	When they need to cry	b
	And they never know why	b
Chorus 2	Doesn't anybody tell them	x
	Doesn't anybody see	a
	Doesn't anybody love them	x
	Like you love me?	a
Bridge	Some people ask,	a
	If tears have to fall	b
	Then why take your chances?	a
	Why bother at all?	b
Verse 5	And some people's lives	a
	Are as cold as their lips	b

	They just need to be kissed	b
Chorus 3	Didn't anybody tell them	x
	Didn't anybody see	a
	Didn't anybody love them	x
	Like you love me?	a
	'Cause that's all they need	a

1. SPOTLIGHTING IMPORTANT IDEAS

This is the easiest and most practical use of balancing. When a section has an even number of phrases, the sections stops for a rest along the high wire. The pause allows the spotlight to shine on the last phrase. The first verse of *Some People's Lives* uses the position well.

Verse 1	Some people's lives	a
	Run down like clocks	b
	One day they stop	b
	That's all they've got	b

That's all they've got is the climax of the section. The balancing position allows us to savor it by letting it rest in the spotlight a few seconds.

2. PUSHING ONE SECTION FORWARD INTO ANOTHER SECTION

An odd number of phrases works wonders when you want the audience to hold its breath. Janis and Kye teeter on the wire in verse four, then pause, (gasp) then they step forward into a balanced chorus:

Verse 4	Some people laugh	a
	When they need to cry	b
	And they never know why	b
Chorus	Didn't anybody tell them	x
	Didn't anybody see	a
	Didn't anybody love them	x
	Like you love me?	a

The chorus settles us down, but some tension still remains: three phrases plus four phrases still leaves us a little queasy. The last phrase of the chorus is a question; the problem of loneliness still looms for some people.

3. CONTRASTING ONE SECTION WITH ANOTHER ONE

The first three verses of *Some People's Lives*, are balanced.

Verse 1	Some people's lives	a
	Run down like clocks	b
	One day they stop	b
	That's all they've got	b

Verse 2	Some lives wear out	a
	Like old tennis shoes	b
	No one can use	b
	It's sad but it's true	b

Verse 3	Some people's eyes	a
	Fade like their dream's	b
	Too tired to rise	a
	Too tired to sleep	b

The *contrast* with these balanced sections gives verse four its power. We expected stability. Instead, it totters on the brink for a breathtaking moment:

Verse 4	Some people laugh	a
	When they need to cry	b
	And they never know why	b

The crowd tenses up and begins to sweat. Will she fall . . .

Another way to unbalance a section is to add a phrase. Look again at *The Great Pretender*. Verses one and two are balanced, so we expect verse three to be balanced.

Verse 1

Yes I'm THE GREAT PRETENDER
Pretending that I'm doing well
My need is such, I pretend too much
I'm lonely but no one can tell

Verse 2

> Yes I'm THE GREAT PRETENDER
> Adrift in a world of my own
> I play the game but to my real shame
> You've left me to dream all alone

Verse 3

> Yes I'm THE GREAT PRETENDER
> Just laughing and gay like a clown
> I seem to be what I'm not, you see
> I'm wearing my heart like a crown
> Pretending that you're still around

The extra phrase is a surprise. Of course line four, the balancing position is still a spotlighted power position. But the extra phrase stumbles forward on the wire to turn additional spotlights onto the most important phrase in the song.

Janis and Kye pull the same trick at the end of *Some People's Lives*. The balanced first and second choruses set up the surprise of the third chorus:

Chorus 3	Didn't anybody tell them	x
	Didn't anybody see	a
	Didn't anybody love them	x
	Like you love me?	a
	'Cause that's all they need	a

The crucial idea gets bathed in spotlights.

4. CREATING A NEED FOR A BALANCING SECTION OR PHRASE

The real beauty of *Some People's Lives* is that the two short sections, verses four and five, each prepare us for a headlong pitch to the sawdust. Chorus two left us queasy, since we were still struggling to balance an odd (seven) number of phrases.

	Some people laugh	a
	When they need to cry	b
(unbalancing)	And they never know why	b

| Chorus 2 | Doesn't anybody tell them | x |

Doesn't anybody see	a
Doesn't anybody love them	x
Like you love me?	a

The bridge balances again with an even number of phrases,

Bridge	Some people ask,	a
	If tears have to fall	b
	Then why take your chances?	a
	Why bother at all?	b

but again, verse five loses its balance (the crowd holds its breath . . .):

Verse 5	And some people's lives	a
	Are as cold as their lips	b
(unbalancing)	They just need to be kissed	b

The last chorus tries to get home, but seems to end short of the platform:

Chorus 3	Didn't anybody tell them	x
	Didn't anybody see	a
	Didn't anybody love them	x
	Like you love me?	a

The crowd remains restless. Things still wobble on the high wire. The bridge/verse/chorus last system certainly did need something more, a need set up by the unbalanced three-phrase verses. Something more finally arrives, in spades: "Cause that's all they need."

Spotlights blaze onto the extra phrase as it balances the entire last system with an even number of phrases (twelve), and steps onto the platform at the other side of the high-wire journey. We breathe a sigh of satisfaction and relief, not only because we have arrived, but because the trip has been fraught with danger and the result has been so satisfying. The last phrase stands firm and strong in the carefully prepared balancing position and delivers its message forcefully: Love is all you need. The crowd goes wild.

You can try this stuff yourself. First try some simple balancing and unbalancing of single sections. Take something like:

> Eenie meenie minee moe
> Catch a tiger by the toe
> If he hollers let him go
> Eenie meenie minee moe

Add a phrase:

> Eenie meenie minee moe
> Catch a tiger by the toe
> Take him to a picture show
> If he hollers let him go
> Eenie meenie minee moe

Take one away:

> Eenie meenie minee moe
> Catch a tiger by the toe
> If he hollers let him go

or maybe:

> Eenie meenie minee moe
> Catch a tiger by the toe
> Eenie meenie minee moe

EXERCISE

Pick a couple of your own lyrics and try it. Then take the next step and surprise us by unbalancing a section we expected to be balanced. Set up the surprise by starting with a balanced section:

> Eenie meenie minee moe
> Catch a tiger by the toe
> Take him to a picture show
> Eenie meenie minee moe

Eenie meenie minee may
If he hollers make him pay
Fifty dollars every day

The technique works best in lyrics with at least three verses. Try it, taking small steps at first, and advancing further until you can work without a net.

Chapter Seventeen

Song Forms:
(Im)Potent Packages

ong form should be your friend, helping you deliver your message with power. But too often, an inefficient or inappropriate form weakens your message, weights it down, and drags it helpless and sagging into the dust. Beware, O beware of song form. Consider it carefully before you choose.

Verse/verse/chorus/verse/verse/chorus is a common but relatively impotent song form. We've all used it, but, if your experience is anything like mine, too often you've gotten mixed results. This song form probably attracts more of the dreaded "seems too long" comment from friends, co-writers, publishers, producers and even mothers than any other.

I know. I know. There have been some great songs written in this form, so why pick on such a successful form? What makes it inefficient?

Simple. V/v/ch/v/v/ch repeats the same melody, chords, phrase lengths and rhyme schemes four times. Four times is a lot. You risk boring your listener when you make four trips through the same structure. Your verses, especially the crucial fourth verse, had better be *very* interesting to risk all that repetition. At best, if your message is powerful and compelling, the v/v/ch/v/v/ch song form won't get in the way, but at worst, you risk it working against effective delivery of your message.

Look at this version of Jim Rushing's *Slow Healing Heart*, arranged as a v/v/ch/v/v/ch lyric:

Verse 1

When I left I left walking wounded
I made my escape from the rain
Still a prisoner of hurt
I had months worth of work
Freeing my mind of the pain

Verse 2

I had hours of sitting so lonely
Singing sad songs in the dark
Feeling my days
Slipping away
Weak is a SLOW HEALING HEART

Chorus

A SLOW HEALING HEART
Is dying to mend
Longing for love
Lonely again
When a spirit is broken
And the memories start
Nothing moves slower
Than a SLOW HEALING HEART

Using two verses before the chorus runs a small risk.
Sometimes publishers (bless their hearts) might say "takes too
long to get to the chorus." But here the problem comes more from
"commercial considerations" than boredom.

After the chorus, verse three starts the second system:

Verse 3

How I prayed for blind faith to lead me
To places where I'm not afraid
Now I'm doing fine
Both in body and mind
But some hurts take longer to fade

Now the crucial fourth verse. Here's where you run the risk
of making the song seem too long.

Verse 4

> There's a part of me still on the lookout
> Alert for those cutting remarks
> Looks that are sweet
> Soon will cause you to bleed
> Weak is a SLOW HEALING HEART

Chorus

> A SLOW HEALING HEART
> Is dying to mend
> Longing for love
> Lonely again
> When a spirit is broken
> And the memories start
> Nothing moves slower
> Than a SLOW HEALING HEART

Go back and read the entire lyric without the interruptions. Does it seem too long? Maybe, maybe not. The answer can vary for individual listeners. All I know is that it's a risk—even if verse four is killer, it's still a risk. If you can avoid the risk effectively, you should. There are three risk-avoidance techniques outlined in this chapter. Get familiar with all of them.

First Risk-Avoidance Technique

Try dumping a verse. Of course, this is not as easy as it sounds, because unless you've written a real dead dog for one of your verses, you probably need at least some of the material in each one. So try to select the most important stuff, on a sort of "best of" principle, and distill one verse from two. Let's try it with verses three and four:

Verse 3

> How I prayed for blind faith to lead me
> To places where I'm not afraid
> Now I'm doing fine
> Both in body and mind
> But some hurts take longer to fade

Verse 4

There's a part of me still on the lookout
Alert for those cutting remarks
Looks that are sweet
Soon will cause you to bleed
Weak is a SLOW HEALING HEART

How about this as a distilled verse:

Verse 3

There's a part of me still on the lookout
Alert for cutting remarks
But the sweetest of words
Only sharpen the hurt
Weak is a SLOW HEALING HEART

Or how about this?

Verse 3

How I prayed for blind faith to lead me
Away from those cutting remarks
Now I'm doing fine
Both in body and mind
But weak is a SLOW HEALING HEART

STOP Go back and substitute each one into the lyric. Read the whole thing together. Why did you keep reading? Go back and read the lyric with each distilled verse.

This resulting verse/verse/chorus/verse/chorus song form is more streamlined. It gives the second chorus a boost by seeming to get to it early—a distinct advantage. And often the distilled verse is stronger than the two separate verses it came from.

EXERCISE

What do you think of my distilled verses? Did I lose too much, or did I keep the necessary stuff? You try it. Distill the original verses three and four into one verse of the same structure. Remember to end the verse with the refrain: *Weak is a slow healing heart.*

Second Risk-Avoidance Technique

Turn one of the verses into a bridge, making the overall form: v/v/ch/v/ch/br/ch.

Be careful with this option. A bridge is a contrasting element, both in structure and in content. You'll have to change both the structure and the kind of information you give.

Maybe this will work:

Verse 3

There's a part of me still on the lookout
Alert for those cutting remarks
Looks that are sweet
Soon will cause you to bleed
Weak is a SLOW HEALING HEART

Chorus

A SLOW HEALING HEART
Is dying to mend
Longing for love
Lonely again
When a spirit is broken
And the memories start
Nothing moves slower
Than a SLOW HEALING HEART

Bridge

I pray that someday
I won't be afraid
But some hurts take longer to fade

Chorus

A SLOW HEALING HEART
Is dying to mend
Longing for love
Lonely again
When a spirit is broken
And the memories start

> Nothing moves slower
> Than a SLOW HEALING HEART

The move to future tense in the bridge helps shift away from the verse material. Shorter lines and a three-line unbalanced section, rhyming AAA change the structure.

STOP Again, go back and read the whole song in the new form. Whad'ya think?

EXERCISE

Now *you* come up with your own bridge.

Third Risk-Avoidance Technique

Keep all the lines, but restructure both verses into a single unit. Of course, this means more than not skipping a space between verses on your lyric sheet. It means changing the form of verse two so it doesn't repeat verse one. Here's the actual lyric by Jim Rushing:

SLOW HEALING HEART

Verse 1

> When I left I left walking wounded
> I made my escape from the rain
> Still a prisoner of hurt
> I had months worth of work
> Freeing my mind of the pain
> I had hours of sitting alone in the dark
> Listening to sad songs and coming apart
> Lord knows I made crying an art
> Weak is a SLOW HEALING HEART

Chorus

> A SLOW HEALING HEART
> Is dying to mend
> Longing for love
> Lonely again
> When a spirit is broken

And the memories start
Nothing moves slower
Than a SLOW HEALING HEART

Verse 2

How I prayed for blind faith to lead me
To places where I'm not afraid
Now I'm doing fine
Both in body and mind
But some hurts take longer to fade
There's a part of my feelings ever on guard
Against looks that are tender and words that are hard
I still remember those cutting remarks
Weak is a SLOW HEALING HEART

Chorus

A SLOW HEALING HEART
Is dying to mend
Longing for love
Lonely again
When a spirit is broken
And the memories start
Nothing moves slower
Than a SLOW HEALING HEART

Look how the verse structure works:

	stresses	rhyme
When I left I left walking wounded	3 +	x
I made my escape from the rain	3	a
Still a prisoner of hurt	2	b
I had months worth of work	2	b
Freeing my mind of the pain	3	a
I had hours of sitting alone in the dark	4	c
Listening to sad songs and coming apart	4	c
Lord knows I made crying an art	4	c
Weak is a SLOW HEALING HEART	3	c

The front half is basic common meter, in three-quarter time, with a rhyme acceleration in the third line. The back half moves two by two in four-stress couplets, creating a whole different feel (which will force a musical change). Jim Rushing creates two interesting, unified verses rather than four helpings of the same structure. Big difference.

Any of these three risk-avoidance techniques solve the problem created by the verse/verse/chorus/verse/verse/chorus form. They will help structure work for you, rather than risking songs that seem too long. Even if every line of all four verses is to die for, you can reorganize them into a form that delivers power rather than sags. All it takes is time, energy and most important, focus on the importance of potent song form. It's worth the work.

Chapter Eighteen

Song Forms:
(Im)Potent Packages II

ored? Try a little variety. That was the principle behind the last chapter, where we looked at the verse/verse/chorus, verse/verse/chorus form.

Here I want to look at another common form—one that also risks boredom, or at least doesn't work real hard to make your lyrics more exciting. verse/chorus, verse/chorus, verse/chorus. Here's a sample:

LOVE HER OR LEAVE HER TO ME
You're living with a woman you ain't true to
Playin' round but keep her hanging on
If you don't want her let me have her
You won't believe how fast I'll grab her
You'll hardly even notice that she's gone

LOVE HER OR LEAVE HER TO ME
Keep her or let her go free
Don't go two-timing her
'Less you're resigning her
LOVE HER OR LEAVE HER TO ME

You're out all night while she's alone without you
Just for fun she calls me on the phone
She comes to me, I play the friend
I know she'll love me in the end
As long as you keep leaving her alone

LOVE HER OR LEAVE HER TO ME
Keep her or let her go free
Don't go two-timing her
'Less you're resigning her
LOVE HER OR LEAVE HER TO ME

Well I guess some men got no appreciation
They never see the finer things in life
When they leave the best behind 'em
Someone else is bound to find 'em
Won't be long she's someone else's wife

LOVE HER OR LEAVE HER TO ME
Keep her or let her go free
Don't go two-timing her
'Less you're resigning her
LOVE HER OR LEAVE HER TO ME

Not a bad lyric. It chugs along nicely for two verse/chorus systems, developing its ideas with light, cute structure. The third system, however, seems to fall a little flat, not so much for what it says, but because we've seen its structure twice before. There's nothing wrong with the form—the form just doesn't help add interest. Let's look at some options to use instead of this third verse/chorus system.

Option 1: The most obvious boredom quencher is to insert a contrasting section—a bridge—between the second and third system. As usual, the contrast should be total. The structure of the bridge should be different from the verse and chorus structures: a different rhyme scheme, different number of lines, different line lengths. It should also say something different.

When you're writing a bridge, start by looking at what you've already said, then look for a missing piece. In this case, we know the speaker wants the wife, and that the husband is fooling around. We know the wife calls the speaker and that the speaker has plans. But we don't know what makes her so desirable. This might be an interesting angle, especially since the third verse starts:

Well, I guess some men got no appreciation
They never see the finer things in life . .

EXERCISE

A bridge focusing on her qualities would lead smoothly into the third verse. I'll leave this bridge to you. Start by making a list of her qualities—things she is. Things she does. Draw the list from your own experiences. Do a little Object Writing, diving into your own sense experience:

> *Kicking through the fallen leaves, gold-brown and red. Cheeks flushed and soft, glowing with the afternoon sunlight. You don't speak, I don't dare speak; our shoulders touching, lingering a little, skin electric, breath coming a little faster. You step slowly, patiently, listening to the leaves swirling and dancing in colors as we move together.*

Your Object Writing will create a mood and character for you to respond to, even if none of it finds its way into the bridge. But probably some of it will. Then try a few bridges. Be sure your bridge is a contrasting section. Keep it short and effective. Take some time out and try it.

STOP Simply inserting a bridge is always an option when you need a boredom breaker. Our risk here: The lyric may get a little long, or seem a little long, because it returns to a verse again before the chorus.

Option 2: Which brings up the second option: a verse/chorus form that stops with two verse/chorus systems, creates a bridge as a contrasting system, then moves directly to a chorus: verse/chorus, verse/chorus, bridge/chorus.

Again, be careful. A bridge isn't a verse—it doesn't do the same job or use the same structure. It is, by definition, a contrasting section. Verses usually develop plot. A chorus usually steps away, comments on or summarizes the verses. In our lyric, the verses develop the situation, the chorus gives a warning. A bridge will have to take a different angle:

You're living with a woman you ain't true to

Playin' round but keep her hanging on
If you don't want her let me have her
You won't believe how fast I'll grab her
You'll hardly even notice that she's gone

LOVE HER OR LEAVE HER TO ME
Keep her or let her go free
Don't go two-timing her
'Less you're resigning her
LOVE HER OR LEAVE HER TO ME

You're out all night while she's alone without you
Just for fun she calls me on the phone
She comes to me, I play the friend
I know she'll love me in the end
As long as you keep leaving her alone

LOVE HER OR LEAVE HER TO ME
Keep her or let her go free
Don't go two-timing her
'Less you're resigning her
LOVE HER OR LEAVE HER TO ME

Leave the finest things behind, an'
Someone else is bound to find 'em

LOVE HER OR LEAVE HER TO ME
Keep her or let her go free
Don't go two-timing her
'Less you're resigning her
LOVE HER OR LEAVE HER TO ME

Neat.

EXERCISE

You might even be able to substitute the bridge you wrote for the one I wrote. Try it.

Option 3: If you can't translate your third verse into a bridge—say that you really need that third idea as a verse—try a form that thrives on three-idea development: the AABA verse/refrain form.

This song form has been around a long time, mostly because it works so well. Let's try it for our three verse lyric, using the title as a refrain.

> You're living with a woman you ain't true to
> You play around, she sits home faithfully
> If you don't want her let me have her
> Wait and see how fast I grab her
> LOVE HER OR LEAVE HER TO ME
>
> While you're out she gets a little lonesome
> What to do, she's got her evenings free
> She calls me up, I play the friend
> I know she'll love me in the end
> LOVE HER OR LEAVE HER TO ME
>
> Boy just keep your blinders on
> You'll never notice when she's gone
>
> I'm glad some men got no appreciation
> The finest things are just too hard to see
> You just keep two-timing her
> Soon you'll be resigning her
> LOVE HER OR LEAVE HER TO ME

Not bad. Clean and effective in AABA.

An AABA song form is effective because it creates a strong sense of resolution when it moves back to the third verse. The first two verses define "home base," then the bridge takes you away from home—away from the familiar structure. When you come back to the third verse, you come back home to familiar territory. It's a real homecoming, seeing the old neighborhood again after a long trip. The tension created by moving away has been resolved.

An AABA's last system is actually bridge/verse, providing a

nice contrast to the opening verses, as well as sponsoring the homecoming parade.

The temptation to write verse/chorus, verse/chorus, verse/chorus is sometimes strong. Resist it. Look instead for forms that present your ideas in more potent packages.

Chapter Nineteen

Process

My friend Bob Nicksic calls. "Got an idea," he says. "You'll love it. It's about a little girl whose parents fight all the time. Whenever they do, she goes into this fantasy world and sings a little song." Pause. "You'll never guess what."

Right. Like I'm going to guess. *"We will, we will rock you?"* I offer.

"Nope."

"Was I close?"

"She sells sea shells! Neat, huh?"

It was weird, not that that ever stops me. But *She sells sea shells?* "Hmmm," I say.

"No. Think about it. I've got some ideas for verses. Listen."

I press *record* on my answering machine. Here's what he gives me:

Planted in the hallway
Hands over her ears
Shaken by the shouting
Growing wise beyond her years

Daddy's voice is thunder
Mommy's voice is rain
She's too scared not to watch
the hurricane

And then She Sells Sea Shells
Cause her mind can't handle any more

So She Sells Sea Shells
On the Shore

She knows daddy's leaving
But this time he says good-bye
Mommy's chest is heaving
This time she doesn't cry

Daddy bends to kiss her
Sea spray on his face
. . . . ?
. . . . ?

Yup, pretty weird. But there was something about it— the sort of spooky that slips in when you're not looking. It was slipping in. Besides, picture a singer in the studio getting to the chorus and stiffening for the tongue twister. Better yet, picture people trying to sing along. Irresistible. It appealed to the sadist in me.

"OK, OK," I say. "I'll sit with it and see what happens." I need to get the lay of the land. Time for a little Object Writing. I think the most productive place to look is at the title, since that's the centerpiece of the song.

Sea Shells

Buried, scooping sand with little mouths like front loaders; Rrrrr of the ocean their motors as they excavate tunnels, trenches, digging to China. Bodies heaped on broken bodies, clattering as waves break and wash over them, polishing and shining, smooth and tumbling. Pick one up, glistening in the sun, rings etched in spirals circling deeper and deeper, little whirlpools sucking, letting me float and spin dizzy like rolling down a grassy hill, the trees in green blurs appearing and disappearing humming in my ears, ringing like waves, like listening to the ocean in a shell. Hold it up, can you hear the ocean. No, the sounds of infinite space tucked in spirals, lost planets bobbing and sinking, the chill and emptiness. Wrap your arms around yourself. There is no warmth or comfort here, winds churning, waves tumbling, tides rolling like huge voices back and forth between continents, sea foam spilling in spirals circling and crashing over shells, crushing them to sand and dust, building into dunes, shifting , disappearing, piling up again.

Not that I'll use it all, or even any of it. The process helps me find out what I have to offer that originates from my own unique sense experiences. The closer I stay to my senses, the more real and effective my writing will be. The front loaders are out of my childhood and may not be helpful in the scene Bob gave me. I like the shells digging to China. The carnage on the beaches and the trenches could well lead to a World War I scene. The spirals etched in the shells may be useful, since the song seems concerned with the consequences for the girl of the parents' break-up. Listening to the shell is a means of escape, though in this world the escape isn't a prosperous one. I like the tides as a metaphor for the parents' voices. The dunes are nice.

CREATE A WORKSHEET

Maybe some useful stuff.

Before I look at the lyric, let's try an abbreviated work sheet for additional stimulation. I want to find the sonic lay of the land for the key words so far: sea, shells, shore, sand, tide.

Sea has no final consonant, so we'll look at perfect rhymes, then additive rhymes.

Debris has wonderful possibilities. Think about a beach scene and let it echo through your own senses and imagination.

I'll pass on three syllable adverbs like breathlessly. First, I'm not a real fan of adverbs in lyrics', second, rhyming the secondary stress with a primary stress sounds awkward. Ditto for three syllable nouns like *memory* and *rhapsody.* I'll stick to words ending on a primary accent.

Disagree isn't bad in this context, but probably not very evocative. I think it's already shown in the verse about thunder and rain. *Free* is overused. No thanks. You've never used *plea* in your life unless you've been in court. Why use it in a lyric just to get a rhyme? *Referee* is tempting, but it takes me somewhere I don't want to be in this song. *Refugee* is terrific. So, I found two stimulating perfect rhymes, *debris* and *refugee*. On to additive rhymes.

Remember, the less sound you add, the closer the rhyme. The least possible sound comes from the voiced plosives, b, d, and g. Nothing under *eb. Recede* is nice. *Seaweed* is possible. Maybe *bleed.* Nothing helpful under *eg.*

On to the unvoiced plosives, p, k, and t. *Deep* and *sleep.* Where do they take you? *Streak* gives me a beach sky at sunset. Perhaps *streaked.* I'm a sucker for *bittersweet,* though I don't see what's sweet in this circumstance. Maybe *retreat* for the waves' ebb and flow.

So here are our rhymes for *sea*: debris, refugee, recede, weeds, bleed, deep, sleep, streaked, retreat.

We'll look up perfect and additive rhymes for shell. Additives are particularly effective because *l,* together with the vowel, make all the sonic connection you'll ever need.

Swell, as in ocean swell. If I could get swelling around the eyes too, so much the better. *Hell* is too dramatic—it's one of those words that seems to mean so much more than it conveys. Like *soul.* Avoid those clunkers. *Carousel* has the circles and childhood. Maybe, though it seems a little off-center for our beach scene.

That's it for perfect rhyme.

Now browse in the rhyming dictionary through short e + l + anything else. All I can find is *withheld* and *help.*

OK. Try consonance rhymes, since we're dealing with *l.* (Change the vowel and keep the final consonants—remember?) Stay with closely related vowel sounds, either short a or short *i.* Nothing under short a + l. Short *i* looks better: *chill, spilled.*

Here's our rhyme column for *shell*: swell, carrousel, help, chill, spilled.

Shore ends in another strong consonant. We'll look at perfect rhyme, additive rhyme and consonance rhyme. This time you let each word carry you into its possibilities: roar, pour, storm, outworn, torn, blur, search, submerged, curled.

For *sand* we'll look at perfect rhyme and family rhyme (since the consonants after the vowel belong to phonetic families) and subtractive rhyme (dropping either consonant after the vowel).

I find nothing interesting under perfect rhyme except the tired old hand/understand/command nonsense.

Let's subtract d, since it's the least noticeable sound. Nothing good. Maybe *ran.*

Let's substitute for *d* from the plosive family (b, d, g, p, t, k): *chant.*

Substitute for *n* from the nasal family (m, n, ng): *slammed, stamped.*

Continue through the rest of the short a + n columns: *inheritance.*

Our results: *sand*: ran, chants, slammed, stamped, inheritance.

Not bad. Our last word, *tide,* ends with a plosive. If it were plural, *tides,* it would also contain members of the fricative family (f, th, s, sh, ch, v, th, z, zh, j) after the vowel. Lots of places to look. Perfect rhymes: *glide, slide.*

Into the plosive family: *inscribed* (patterns etched), *flight, harbor light.*

Go to the plural, *tides:* subtract *d: sacrifice.*

Look at the *s* family: *still life, revived, rise, arise.*

Tide: glide, slide, inscribed, flight, harbor light, sacrifice, still life, revived, rise, arise.

So here's our abbreviated worksheet:

1. sea
2. shells
3. shore
4. sand
5. tide

1. sea	**2. shells**	**3. shore**	**4. sand**	**5. tide**
debris	swell	roars	ran	glide
refugee	carousel	pour	chants	slide
recede	help	storm	slammed	inscribed
weeds	chill	outrworn	stamped	flight
bleed	spilled	torn	inheritance	harbor light
deep		blur		sacrifice
sleep		search		still life
streaked		submerged		revived
retreat		curled		rise, arise

Use the worksheet for reference. Remember, its main purpose is to get additional ideas and pictures. It is a brainstorming device, not a rhyme finding device. It's a nice reference though. Ask Stephen Sondheim. He uses worksheets all the time.

Back to Bob's original ideas.

Round One

Planted in the hallway
Hands over her ears

Shaken by the shouting
Growing wise beyond her years

Daddy's voice is thunder
Mommy's voice is rain
She's too scared not to watch
the hurricane

And then She Sells Sea Shells
Cause her mind can't handle any more
So She Sells Sea Shells
On the Shore

She knows daddy's leaving
But this time he says good-bye
Mommy's chest is heaving
This time she doesn't cry

Daddy bends to kiss her
Sea spray on his face . . .?

Look at the chorus. I don't really know what the verses will end up doing, especially since even the rough verses are incomplete. So I don't want to make too early a commitment to a lot of ideas in the chorus. It's best to keep it streamlined and simple at first. My first job is to make sure the verses set up the title. Additional lines can come along later when I'm sure the title works with the verses. So:

And then She Sells Sea Shells
Cause her mind can't handle any more
So She Sells Sea Shells
On the Shore

becomes

SHE SELLS SEA SHELLS, SHE SELLS SEA SHELLS
SHE SELLS SEA SHELLS BY THE SHORE

The first two verses seem backwards. The reaction is before the action. Try:

> Daddy's voice is thunder
> Mommy's voice is rain
> She's too scared not to watch
> the hurricane

> Planted in the hallway
> Hands over her ears
> Shaken by the shouting
> Growing wise beyond her years

> SHE SELLS SEA SHELLS, SHE SELLS SEA SHELLS
> SHE SELLS SEA SHELLS BY THE SHORE

Better opening. Now look at the line before the chorus—(I call it the trigger line because it releases its meaning into the chorus. Whatever the trigger line says will determine how we see the chorus.)

> Shaken by the shouting
> Growing wise beyond her years . . .

> SHE SELLS SEA SHELLS, SHE SELLS SEA SHELLS
> SHE SELLS SEA SHELLS BY THE SHORE

I don't get the connection. And I want the first chorus to be the clearest of all. So we need a stronger trigger line. How about:

> She hums a tiny melody
> Hands over her ears

> SHE SELLS SEA SHELLS, SHE SELLS SEA SHELLS
> SHE SELLS SEA SHELLS BY THE SHORE

Better, but I still don't quite get the connection. Eureka! How about:

> She hums this tiny melody
> Hands over her ears
>
> SHE SELLS SEA SHELLS, SHE SELLS SEA SHELLS
> SHE SELLS SEA SHELLS BY THE SHORE

Now the chorus *becomes* her tiny melody. It's important to take time to work on your trigger lines. They are power positions, but more important, they are the last thing you hear before you enter your chorus or refrain, so they have extra responsibility. Always take time to check them, the earlier the better.

The chorus seems pretty locked in just the way it is—something the little girl can sing, at least in the first system. A commentary line like " 'Cause her mind can't handle any more," seems inappropriate.

Let's finish the verse. For now, how about:

> Shaken by their shouting
> Wise beyond her years
> She hums this tiny melody
> Hands over her ears

Our whole first song system is:

> Daddy's voice is thunder
> Mama's voice is rain
> She's too scared not to watch
> the hurricane
>
> Shaken by their shouting
> Wise beyond her years
> She hums this tiny melody
> Hands over her ears
>
> SHE SELLS SEA SHELLS, SHE SELLS SEA SHELLS
> SHE SELLS SEA SHELLS BY THE SHORE

It seems to work OK. It sets up the scene, and sets up the chorus pretty clearly. We'll squeeze out the kinks later. Right now there's second verse hell to deal with.

Bob's third verse has the fight turning into a separation. Something unusual is happening:

> She knows daddy's leaving
> But this time he says good-bye
> Mommy's chest is heaving
> This time she doesn't cry

Not bad development. Daddy's leaving should increase her isolation; in fact, it will change her life. So what can we do with daddy's good-bye?

> Daddy bends to kiss her
> Sea spray on his face. . . . ?

I was tempted to start looking for ideas with a rhyme search for *face*, (avoiding some of the ugly possibilities like *that time will not erase* or *gone without a trace*). I would have gone for family rhymes like *safe* or *rage*, or additive or subtractive rhymes like *waste* or *stray*. Even assonance rhymes like *ache* or *rain* would work, since they would provide a sense of a closed section, yet leave it hanging a little bit. Perfectly fine in this context.

But wait a minute: *sea spray on his face?*

Where the hell did the *spray* come from? In my mental picture they're inside. Sure, spray could be a way of saying *tears*, but if there is no place for the spray to come from, it's confusing. A metaphor has to be grounded in something real. If they were on the beach, "sea spray on his face" would be just fine. It could be both what it is, plus more. Remember to ground your metaphors in reality. They must have a legitimate place in the context. So I've got to decide. Are they in the house or at the ocean? I can't just assume that my mental picture is everybody's mental picture. I've got to make it everybody's mental picture.

Secondly, it seems like this verse has got to be the little girl's verse. It seems like a waste of space to let daddy linger. He said good-bye three lines ago—get him out. We have to set up the little girl's isolation. How about this for verse four:

> Shuts the door behind her
> Escaping to her room

Days stretch out before her
Like sand and shifting dunes

She's isolated inside her room. Let's look at the trigger:

Days stretch out before her
Like sand and shifting dunes

SHE SELLS SEA SHELLS, SHE SELLS SEA SHELLS
SHE SELLS SEA SHELLS BY THE SHORE

Now the little girl becomes *she* in the chorus. She's in her room
(in my head) with the sands of time (ick, though it's suggested
rather than stated, which is actually pretty neat) stretching out
before her. Plus we get the overlay of the little song she sings in
the first chorus. Not bad.

So here's system two so far:

She knows daddy's leaving
But this time he says good-bye
Mommy's chest is heaving
This time she doesn't cry

Shuts the door behind her
Escaping to her room
Days stretch out before her
Like sand and shifting dunes

SHE SELLS SEA SHELLS, SHE SELLS SEA SHELLS
SHE SELLS SEA SHELLS BY THE SHORE

The whole thing:

SHE SELLS SEA SHELLS (VERSION 1)
Daddy's voice is thunder
Mama's voice is rain
She's too scared not to watch
the hurricane

Shaken by their shouting
Wise beyond her years

She hums a tiny melody
Hands over her ears

SHE SELLS SEA SHELLS, SHE SELLS SEA SHELLS
SHE SELLS SEA SHELLS BY THE SHORE

She knows daddy's leaving
But this time he says good-bye
Mommy's chest is heaving
This time she doesn't cry

Shuts the door behind her
Escaping to her room
Days stretch out before her
Like sand and shifting dunes

SHE SELLS SEA SHELLS, SHE SELLS SEA SHELLS
SHE SELLS SEA SHELLS BY THE SHORE

I like common meter for the verses. Sort of nursery rhymish with a lot of flexibility musically. I thought Bob would be impressed. I call back. "What d'ya think?"

"Works OK. But who's *she* in the first verse? Sounds like the mother is the one that's scared, not the daughter. And who isn't crying in the third verse?"

Right. "Call you back."

Round Two

SHE SELLS SEA SHELLS (VERSION 2)
Daddy's voice is thunder
Mama's voice is rain
Baby's too scared not to watch
the hurricane

Shaken by their shouting
Wise beyond her years
She *sings* this tiny melody (rather than *hums*, since the chorus has
    words)
Hands *cupped* over ears

SHE SELLS SEA SHELLS, SHE SELLS SEA SHELLS
SHE SELLS SEA SHELLS, *SEA SHELLS* BY THE SHORE (I was
tapping in threes, and the repetition felt right and sounded good.)

Daddy says he's leaving (more direct)
This time it's good-bye (better rhythm match; more direct)
Mama's chest is heaving
Too upset to cry (clearer reference to mama; more elegantly stated)

Baby shuts the door behind her
Escaping to her room
Days stretch out before her
Like sand and shifting dunes

SHE SELLS SEA SHELLS, SHE SELLS SEA SHELLS
SHE SELLS SEA SHELLS, SEA SHELLS BY THE SHORE

I really liked her hands cupped over her ears, like she was listening to the ocean rather than the fight. I think *sings* sets up the first chorus even better. And it's clear who the daughter is and who the mother is. I call back. "What d'ya think?"

"Not a bad sketch."

I think, "Sketch? Sketch! Hey, this is *great* stuff! True art . . .". "Thanks," I mumble. "What else do you think it needs?" Like it could be improved on.

"Some of the lines are a little weird. Could be more elegantly stated," he says, tossing one of my favorite critiquing phrases back in my face. I hate being on the receiving end of those little grenades.

Back to it. I thought maybe, in addition to looking for better lines, I'd take a shot at a bridge that looked ahead to her later life—sort of the consequences of her childhood isolation.

Round Three

Here's attempt number three. (Instead of looking only at the re-written lines, read it all the way through each time to immerse yourself in it. Otherwise the changes won't make much sense or difference.)

SHE SELLS SEA SHELLS (VERSION 3)

Daddy's voice is thunder
Mama's voice is rain
Baby's scared to watch (the double negative was too complicated)
the hurricane

Shaken by their shouting
Choking back her tears (wise beyond her years was a cliché, plus it led
    to a dead end)
She sings this tiny melody
Hands cupped over ears

SHE SELLS SEA SHELLS, SHE SELLS SEA SHELLS
SHE SELLS SEA SHELLS, SEA SHELLS BY THE SHORE

Daddy says he's leaving
This time it's good-bye
Mama's chest is heaving
Too upset to cry

Baby stumbles down the hall (it wasn't clear what door she shut; better
    rhythmic match)
Escaping to her room
Years stretch out before her (Takes us deeper and further into her life)
Like sand and shifting dunes

SHE SELLS SEA SHELLS, SHE SELLS SEA SHELLS
SHE SELLS SEA SHELLS, SEA SHELLS BY THE SHORE

Patterns etched those years before (like patterns on seashells)
Circle through her life
She wanders down the beach alone
watching tides

SHE SELLS SEA SHELLS, SHE SELLS SEA SHELLS
SHE SELLS SEA SHELLS, SEA SHELLS BY THE SHORE

    The bridge sort of fell out like that. It seemed like the right idea, but something bothered me about it. Structurally, it was the bridge from Paul Simon's *Still Crazy After All These Years*, with the telltale short last line. But how bad could that be? I love that bridge. No one would know, unless I told them . . .

Maybe the last line could be longer to slow everything down, like the bridge in Paul Simon's *Train in the Distance*. How bad could that be? I love that bridge too. No one would know, unless I told them . . . Plus, it would give me more room to "state it more elegantly."

> Patterns etched those years before
> Circle through her life
> She wanders down the beach alone
> *Searching through the leavings of the tides* (this came from *debris* in the
> worksheet)

At which point it hits me. This bridge can't be in common meter—the verses already are. I'd fallen into the same old trap of locking into a pattern mentally and writing it automatically. C'mon stupid, a bridge is supposed to contrast, and you've got to make a difference right away, at the first line. I liked the five-stress last line, so I tried it in the first line, and decided on a three-line bridge for a little asymmetry:

> Years have etched their patterns in her life
> She walks the beach alone
> Searching through the leavings of the tides

Better. I hope Bob likes it. Sometimes my preference for asymmetry drives him nuts. Go back and read version three completely, with the new bridge.

Before I call, one more thing. I've written at least three articles insisting that you check every lyric you write from all points of view. This one was a third person narrative. I have to check out first person narrative, with the little girl as the speaker:

SHE SELLS SEA SHELLS (VERSION 4)

Daddy's voice is thunder
Mama's voice is rain
I'm too scared to watch
the hurricane

Shaken by their shouting
Choking back *my* tears
I sing this tiny melody
Hands cupped over ears

SHE SELLS SEA SHELLS, SHE SELLS SEA SHELLS
SHE SELLS SEA SHELLS, SEA SHELLS BY THE SHORE

Daddy says he's leaving
This time it's good-bye
Mama's chest is heaving
Too upset to cry

Stumb*ling* down the hall*way*
Escap*ing* to my room
Years stretch out before me
Like sand and shifting dunes

SHE SELLS SEA SHELLS, SHE SELLS SEA SHELLS
SHE SELLS SEA SHELLS, SEA SHELLS BY THE SHORE

Years have etched their patterns in my life
I walk the beach alone
Searching through the leavings of the tides

SHE SELLS SEA SHELLS, SHE SELLS SEA SHELLS
SHE SELLS SEA SHELLS, SEA SHELLS BY THE SHORE

Did you read it all the way through? It doesn't work very well, does it? There's got to be a tense change for it to make sense. The little girl has to be looking back from adulthood:

SHE SELLS SEA SHELLS (VERSION 5)
Daddy's voice *was* thunder
Mama's voice *was* rain
I was scared to watch
the hurricane

Shaken by their shouting
Choking back my tears

I'd sing this tiny melody
Hands cupped over ears

SHE SELLS SEA SHELLS, SHE SELLS SEA SHELLS
SHE SELLS SEA SHELLS, SEA SHELLS BY THE SHORE

Daddy *said* he's leaving
This time it's good-bye
Mama's chest *was* heaving
Too upset to cry

Stumbling down the hallway
Escaping to my room
Years *stretched* out before me
Like sand and shifting dunes

SHE SELLS SEA SHELLS, SHE SELLS SEA SHELLS
SHE SELLS SEA SHELLS, SEA SHELLS BY THE SHORE

Years have etched their patterns in my life
I walk the beach alone
Searching through the leavings of the tides

SHE SELLS SEA SHELLS, SHE SELLS SEA SHELLS
SHE SELLS SEA SHELLS, SEA SHELLS BY THE SHORE

The move from past tense verses to a present tense bridge works. And each chorus has her cupping her hands over her ears and singing her little song, even as an adult. Kind of a spooky effect. This point of view is a contender.

Now let's try it as a second person narrative, on the model of Bob Seger's *The Fire Inside*. Read it all the way through.

SHE SELLS SEA SHELLS (VERSION 6)

Daddy's voice is thunder
Mama's voice is rain
You're too scared to watch
the hurricane

Shaken by their shouting
Choking back your tears
You sing this tiny melody
Hands cupped over ears

SHE SELLS SEA SHELLS, SHE SELLS SEA SHELLS
SHE SELLS SEA SHELLS, SEA SHELLS BY THE SHORE

Daddy says he's leaving
This time it's good-bye
Mama's chest is heaving
Too upset to cry

You stumble down the hallway
Escaping to your room
Years stretch out before you
Like sand and shifting dunes

SHE SELLS SEA SHELLS, SHE SELLS SEA SHELLS
SHE SELLS SEA SHELLS, SEA SHELLS BY THE SHORE

Years have etched their patterns in your life
You walk the beach alone
Searching through the leavings of the tides

SHE SELLS SEA SHELLS, SHE SELLS SEA SHELLS
SHE SELLS SEA SHELLS, SEA SHELLS BY THE SHORE

Oops. The chorus has to stay in third person. Period. That's the attraction of the song. But the third person chorus doesn't work very well with "you," especially the second and third times. Goodbye to second person narrative.

So it's between third and first person narrative. Close call. Look at versions three and version five side by side:

VERSION 5	**VERSION 6**
Daddy's voice was thunder	Daddy's voice is thunder
Mama's voice was rain	Mama's voice is rain
I was scared to watch	Baby's scared to watch
the hurricane	the hurricane

Shaken by their shouting	Shaken by their shouting
Choking back my tears	Choking back her tears
I'd sing this tiny melody	She sings this tiny melody
Hands cupped over ears	Hands cupped over ears

SHE SELLS SEA SHELLS, SHE SELLS SEA SHELLS
SHE SELLS SEA SHELLS, SEA SHELLS BY THE SHORE

Daddy said he's leaving	Daddy says he's leaving
This time it's good-bye	This time it's good-bye
Mama's chest was heaving	Mama's chest is heaving
Too upset to cry	Too upset to cry

Stumbling down the hallway	Baby stumbles down the hall
Escaping to my room	Escaping to her room
Years stretched out before me	Years stretch out before her
Like sand and shifting dunes	Like sand and shifting dunes

SHE SELLS SEA SHELLS, SHE SELLS SEA SHELLS
SHE SELLS SEA SHELLS, SEA SHELLS BY THE SHORE

Years have etched their	Years have etched their
patterns in my life	patterns in her life
I walk the beach alone	She walks the beach alone
Searching through the	Searching through the
leavings of the tides	leavings of the tides

SHE SELLS SEA SHELLS, SHE SELLS SEA SHELLS
SHE SELLS SEA SHELLS, SEA SHELLS BY THE SHORE

Make your own list of pros and cons. I like the intimacy of first person. Here, however, we lose some immediacy in past tense. The distancing of third person can be effective, but we really don't feel that much distance because the present tense verses are so immediate.

What locks in my decision is the way the third person bridge flows into the chorus. *She* in the bridge becomes *she* in the chorus! Neat. So it's third person, just like we started.

STOP Is there any reason to try a version of third person with the verses in past tense? Yup. Process. Go back to version three and do it.

I don't like it either. It loses our treasured immediacy. So the verses stay in present tense.

One more thing. How about keeping the narrator focused on the little girl the whole song? We could put the bridge in future tense. (Never forget future tense. Sometimes it can work miracles.)

> Years *will* etch their patterns in her life
> She'*ll* walk the beach alone
> Searching through the leavings of the tides
>
> SHE SELLS SEA SHELLS, SHE SELLS SEA SHELLS . . .

A big difference in focus. I really like the future tense. It moves into the present tense chorus just as effectively, and keeps the speaker looking at the little girl in her room. So here's what we've got:

SHE SELLS SEA SHELLS (VERSION 7)

Daddy's voice is thunder
Mama's voice is rain
Baby's scared to watch
the hurricane

Shaken by their shouting
Choking back her tears
She sings this tiny melody
Hands cupped over ears

SHE SELLS SEA SHELLS, SHE SELLS SEA SHELLS
SHE SELLS SEA SHELLS, SEA SHELLS BY THE SHORE

Daddy says he's leaving
This time it's good-bye
Mama's chest is heaving
Too upset to cry

Baby stumbles down the hall
Escaping to her room
Years stretch out before her
Like sand and shifting dunes

SHE SELLS SEA SHELLS, SHE SELLS SEA SHELLS
SHE SELLS SEA SHELLS, SEA SHELLS BY THE SHORE

Years have etched their patterns in her life
She walks the beach alone
Searching through the leavings of the tides

SHE SELLS SEA SHELLS, SHE SELLS SEA SHELLS
SHE SELLS SEA SHELLS, SEA SHELLS BY THE SHORE

There. Point of view and tense check out. Finally, let's look to see how effective the form is. Right now it's verse verse chorus/ verse verse chorus/ bridge chorus.

Hmm. When we get to verse four we've seen the same structure three times before, threatening to make the song feel too long. An impotent form. So what are our options?

Option 1: Dump verse four (or three). That would give us the more streamlined and effective: verse verse chorus/ verse chorus/ bridge chorus. Look at verses three and four. Can we dump one?

Daddy says he's leaving
This time it's good-bye
Mama's chest is heaving
Too upset to cry

Baby stumbles down the hall
Escaping to her room
Years stretch out before her
Like sand and shifting dunes

Try reading from the top, leaving out verse three. She doesn't seem to have a reason to stumble down the hall, nor is there a basis for the dramatic lines

Years stretch out before her
Like sand and shifting dunes

We need to know daddy's leaving.
We can't do without verse four either. We couldn't get into the chorus effectively.

Option 2: Combine verses three and four into one effective verse.

Daddy says he's leaving
This time it's good-bye
Mama's chest is heaving
Too upset to cry

Baby stumbles down the hall
Escaping to her room
Years stretch out before her
Like sand and shifting dunes

Four ideas, each one two lines long. Maybe the bridge can cover the final two lines.

Years stretch out before her
Like sand and shifting dunes

Years will etch their patterns in her life
She'll walk the beach alone
Searching through the leavings of the tides

They're not the same, but let's suppose that the bridge will at least suggest the last two lines' idea. We're left with:

Daddy says he's leaving
This time it's good-bye
Mama's chest is heaving
Too upset to cry

Baby stumbles down the hall
Escaping to her room

Let's get rid of mama's reaction and adjust the rhymes:

SHE SELLS SEA SHELLS (VERSION 8)
Daddy's voice is thunder
Mama's voice is rain
Baby's scared to watch
the hurricane

Shaken by their shouting
Choking back her tears
She sings this tiny melody
Hands cupped over ears

SHE SELLS SEA SHELLS, SHE SELLS SEA SHELLS
SHE SELLS SEA SHELLS, SEA SHELLS BY THE SHORE

Daddy says he's leaving
This time it's good-bye
Baby stumbles to her room
They won't hear her cry (trigger into the chorus)

SHE SELLS SEA SHELLS, SHE SELLS SEA SHELLS
SHE SELLS SEA SHELLS, SEA SHELLS BY THE SHORE

Years will etch their patterns in her life
She'll walk the beach alone
Searching through the leavings of the tides

SHE SELLS SEA SHELLS, SHE SELLS SEA SHELLS
SHE SELLS SEA SHELLS, SEA SHELLS BY THE SHORE

What do you think? Certainly the form is more effective. I miss the picture of mama, its drama. I like the way the bridge fills in for the last two lines of the old verse four though. Let's see what else we can do.

Option 3: Rather than identical verses, change the structure of verses two and four so the same structure doesn't repeat four times. Of course, the structure of verses two and four still match each other. Let's work with the first song system.

Daddy's voice is thunder	x
Mama's voice is rain	a
Baby's scared to watch	x
the hurricane	a
Shaken by their shouting	x
Choking back her tears	b
Hands cupped over ears	b
She sings this tiny song so she can't hear	b

Changing the rhyme scheme and extending the last line gives us a nice contrast with verse one. The two structures are related, but verse two develops and will force musical development as well.

Can we play the same trick in the second song system?

Daddy says he's leaving	x
This time it's good-bye	a
Mama's chest is heaving	x
Too upset to cry	a
Baby stumbles down the hall	x
Escaping to her room	b
Lost inside her childish tune	b
Years stretch out like sand and shifting dunes	b

Not bad. This is the result:

SHE SELLS SEA SHELLS (VERSION 9)

Daddy's voice is thunder
Mama's voice is rain
Baby's scared to watch
the hurricane

Shaken by their shouting
Choking back her tears
Hands cupped over ears
She sings this tiny song so she can't hear

SHE SELLS SEA SHELLS, SHE SELLS SEA SHELLS
SHE SELLS SEA SHELLS, SEA SHELLS BY THE SHORE

Daddy says he's leaving
This time it's good-bye
Mama's chest is heaving
Too upset to cry

Baby stumbles down the hall
Escaping to her room
Lost inside her childish tune
Years stretch out like sand and shifting dunes

SHE SELLS SEA SHELLS, SHE SELLS SEA SHELLS
SHE SELLS SEA SHELLS, SEA SHELLS BY THE SHORE

Years will etch their patterns in her life
She'll walk the beach alone
Searching through the leavings of the tides

SHE SELLS SEA SHELLS, SHE SELLS SEA SHELLS
SHE SELLS SEA SHELLS, SEA SHELLS BY THE SHORE

Option 4: Change verses two and four into transitional sections to go between verse and chorus. Let's extend verse two into two five-stress lines.

Daddy's voice is thunder
Mama's voice is rain
Baby's scared to watch
the hurricane

Cold and shaken, choking back her tears
She sings this song, hands cupped over ears

SHE SELLS SEA SHELLS, SHE SELLS SEA SHELLS
SHE SELLS SEA SHELLS, SEA SHELLS BY THE SHORE

Not bad. How about the second song system?

Daddy says he's leaving
This time it's good-bye
Mama's chest is heaving
Too upset to cry

Baby disappears inside her room
Years stretch out like sand and shifting dunes

SHE SELLS SEA SHELLS, SHE SELLS SEA SHELLS
SHE SELLS SEA SHELLS, SEA SHELLS BY THE SHORE

The transitional sections have the virtue of forcing a strong musical development. Each song system becomes an integrated unit. Here's our result:

SHE SELLS SEA SHELLS (VERSION 10)
Daddy's voice is thunder
Mama's voice is rain
Baby's scared to watch
the hurricane

Cold and shaken, choking back her tears
She sings this song, hands cupped over ears

SHE SELLS SEA SHELLS, SHE SELLS SEA SHELLS
SHE SELLS SEA SHELLS, SEA SHELLS BY THE SHORE

Daddy says he's leaving
This time it's good-bye
Mama's chest is heaving
Too upset to cry

Baby disappears inside her room
Years stretch out like sand and shifting dunes

SHE SELLS SEA SHELLS, SHE SELLS SEA SHELLS
SHE SELLS SEA SHELLS, SEA SHELLS BY THE SHORE

Years will etch their patterns in her life
She'll walk the beach alone
Searching through the leavings of the tides

SHE SELLS SEA SHELLS, SHE SELLS SEA SHELLS
SHE SELLS SEA SHELLS, SEA SHELLS BY THE SHORE

So we've developed three new possibilities, plus the original. Go back and read all four versions and pick a favorite.

VERSION 7

SHE SELLS SEA SHELLS
Daddy's voice is thunder
Mama's voice is rain
Baby's scared to watch
the hurricane

Shaken by their shouting
Choking back her tears
She sings this tiny melody
Hands cupped over ears

VERSION 8

SHE SELLS SEA SHELLS
Daddy's voice is thunder
Mama's voice is rain
Baby's scared to watch
the hurricane

Shaken by their shouting
Choking back her tears
She sings this tiny melody
Hands cupped over ears

SHE SELLS SEA SHELLS, SHE SELLS SEA SHELLS
SHE SELLS SEA SHELLS, SEA SHELLS BY THE SHORE

Daddy says he's leaving
This time it's good-bye
Mama's chest is heaving
Too upset to cry

Baby stumbles down the hall
Escaping to her room
Years streach out before her
Like sand and shifting dunes

Daddy says he's leaving
This time it's good-bye
Baby stumbles to her room
They won't hear her cry

SHE SELLS SEA SHELLS, SHE SELLS SEA SHELLS
SHE SELLS SEA SHELLS, SEA SHELLS BY THE SHORE

Years will etch their patterns in her life
She'll walk the beach alone
Searching through the leavings of the tides

SHE SELLS SEA SHELLS, SHE SELLS SEA SHELLS
SHE SELLS SEA SHELLS, SEA SHELLS BY THE SHORE

VERSION 9

SHE SELLS SEA SHELLS

VERSION 10

SHE SELLS SEA SHELLS

Daddy's voice is thunder
Mama's voice is rain
Baby's scared to watch
the hurricane

Shaken by their shouting

Choking back her tears

Hands cupped over ears
She sings this tiny song so she
can't hear

Daddy's voice is thunder
Mama's voice is rain
Baby's scared to watch
the hurricane

Cold and shaken, choking
back her tears
She sings this song, hands
cupped over ears

SHE SELLS SEA SHELLS, SHE SELLS SEA SHELLS
SHE SELLS SEA SHELLS, SEA SHELLS BY THE SHORE

Daddy says he's leaving
This time it's good-bye
Mama's chest is heaving
Too upset to cry

Baby stumbles down the hall

Escaping to her room

Lost inside her childish tune
Years stretch out like sand and
shifting dunes

Daddy says he's leaving
This time it's good-bye
Mama's chest is heaving
Too upset to cry

Baby disappears inside her
room
Years strech out like sand and
shifting dunes

SHE SELLS SEA SHELLS, SHE SELLS SEA SHELLS
SHE SELLS SEA SHELLS, SEA SHELLS BY THE SHORE

Years will etch their patterns in her life
She'll walk the beach alone
Searching through the leavings of the tides

SHE SELLS SEA SHELLS,
SHE SELLS SEA SHELLS
SHE SELLS SEA SHELLS,
SEA SHELLS BY THE SHORE

Perhaps the final choice is a matter of taste, but the important part is the process—developing alternatives, is what makes the decisions based on taste possible.

Maybe I could have written lines in option three and option four that would have made me like them better, but my choice is number two. I like the way the second verse sets up the chorus both as her little song (with *cry* in the sense of *call*) and as a commentary ("they won't hear her weeping while she sells sea shells"). No, I don't expect everyone to get it, but it's still there resonating and making the emotions richer. Plus, given the last line "they won't hear her cry," "their patterns" in the bridge now refers both to the parents' patterns and the patterns etched by the years.

My next step: Fax Bob. Then call.

Confidently, already salivating at the prospect of watching the blood drain from the demo singer's face when the first chorus comes around, I say, "What d'ya think?"

Silence on his part. Minutes pass.

He clears his throat. Is he trying to torture me? I suddenly understand my students' suffering as I sit in silence looking over and over their lyrics. Finally he says, "A three-line bridge?"

I knew it.

Of course, we're not done. Now the setting process begins and things may change radically. But I'm ready for anything, since I've gone through the process thoroughly.

"Wait till you hear the music I've started for it," he says.

Oh goody. My turn.

AFTERWORD

Well, you did it. Congratulations. Slowing the process down really makes you able to see and learn a lot. Now, a final caution: Don't let all the stuff you've learned block you—don't let it get in the way of your writing.

The difference between writing and rewriting is not a difference in degree, it is a difference in kind. Technical knowledge is invaluable for rewriting, but it is a block for generating ideas. Chapters one, two and three are there to help you generate ideas, so use them as part of your writing process. But hold off using the ideas in the rest of the book until later in the lyric process, when you get to the rewriting stages. Create all the raw material you can, so you'll have something to work with before you plug in the later stuff. If you start worrying about development, form or point of view too early, you probably won't know how to decide, and you'll get blocked. All things in their own time.

Once you get to the later stages, the rewriting, what you *know* is everything. Ideas and techniques become effective polishing tools rather than blocks to creativity. After a while, some of the technical stuff will filter into your bloodstream and will become part of your creative process, but don't force it. This is a lifetime journey, and each ending is a new beginning. Go slow. Have fun.

Pat Pattison
February 20, 1995

INDEX

More Great Books
for Songwriters!